Interactive Reader and Study Guide

D1490152

HOLT

Social Studies
United States History
Beginnings to 1914

HOLT, RINEHART AND WINSTON
A Harcourt Education Company
Orlando • **Austin** • New York • San Diego • London

Copyright © by Holt, Rinehart and Winston.

All rights reserved. No part of this publication may be reproduced or transmitted in any form or by any means, electronic or mechanical, including photocopy, recording, or any information storage and retrieval system, without permission in writing from the publisher.

Teachers using HOLT SOCIAL STUDIES: UNITED STATES HISTORY may photocopy complete pages in sufficient quantities for classroom use only and not for resale.

HOLT and the "Owl Design" are registered trademarks licensed to Holt, Rinehart and Winston, registered in the United States of America and/or other jurisdictions.

Printed in the United States of America

If you have received these materials as examination copies free of charge, Holt, Rinehart and Winston retains title to the materials and they may not be resold. Resale of examination copies is strictly prohibited.

Possession of this publication in print format does not entitle users to convert this publication, or any portion of it, into electronic format.

ISBN 0-03-042654-5

7 8 1409 13 12

4500368787

Contents

Copyright © by Holt, Rinehart and Winston. All rights reserved.

Interactive Reader and Study Guide

Contents

Copyright © by Holt, Rinehart and Winston. All rights reserved.

The World before the Opening of the Atlantic

CHAPTER SUMMARY

The Earliest Americans	Native American Cultures	Trading Kingdoms of West Africa	Europe before Transatlantic Travel
The first Americans migrated to the Americas by crossing the _____ during the last Ice Age.	Several Native American cultures existed in North America before the Europeans came.	By controlling trade, three great kingdoms developed in West Africa. These were the kingdoms of Ghana, Mali, and _____.	The Greeks developed a system of government called _____, in which people rule themselves.
Four early American civilizations were the Olmec, Maya, Aztec, and _____.	The cultures of Native American people varied depending on _____.	A key part of the West African economy was the _____ trade.	After the Black Death, the feudal system weakened and a middle class developed.
	Native American cultures shared beliefs about religion and _____.		The Renaissance was a rebirth of arts and learning.

COMPREHENSION AND CRITICAL THINKING

As you read the section summaries, fill in the blanks in the graphic organizer above and answer the questions below.

1. **Explain** What are cultural areas? How did they shape the ways different Native American peoples developed?

   _____

   _____

2. **Compare and Contrast** How were the societies that existed in the Old and New Worlds before transatlantic travel similar? How were they different?

   _____

   _____

   _____

   _____

Copyright © by Holt, Rinehart and Winston. All rights reserved.

The World before the Opening of the Atlantic

MAIN IDEAS

1. Climate changes allowed Paleo-Indians to begin the first migration to the Americas.
2. Early societies existed in Mesoamerica and South America.

Key Terms and People

Bering Land Bridge a strip of land between Asia and present-day Alaska that was exposed by the lower sea levels of the Ice Age

Paleo-Indians people believed to have crossed the Bering Land Bridge

migration movement of people or animals from one region to another

hunter-gatherers people who obtain food by hunting animals and gathering plants

environments climates and landscapes that surround living things

culture a group's set of common values and traditions

Academic Vocabulary

develop the process of growing or improving

Section Summary

FIRST MIGRATION TO THE AMERICAS

Many scientists believe that the first people arrived in North America during the last Ice Age. At that time the **environment** changed, and large amounts of water froze, forming glaciers. Water levels in the oceans dropped to more than 300 feet lower than they are today. A strip of land called the **Bering Land Bridge** was exposed between Asia and Alaska.

> How did the formation of glaciers during the Ice Age allow for migration to North America?
>
> _____
> _____
> _____

No one knows exactly when or how people crossed into North America, but there is evidence that people called **Paleo-Indians** crossed the bridge to Alaska between 38,000 and 10,000 BC. The **migration** took place over a long time. The descendents of the migrants went as far as the southern tip of South America. These people were **hunter-gatherers,** people who hunted animals and gathered wild plants for food. The environments they settled in created Native American societies.

> Do scientists know exactly when the Paleo-Indians crossed into North America?
>
> _____
> _____

Copyright © by Holt, Rinehart and Winston. All rights reserved.

Interactive Reader and Study Guide

EARLY MESOAMERICAN AND SOUTH AMERICAN SOCIETIES

Some of the earliest American **cultures** arose in Mesoamerica, a region that includes the southern part of what is now Mexico and northern Central America. The Olmec **developed** the earliest known civilization in Mesoamerica around 1200 BC. The Olmec are known for their stone buildings and sculptures. By 400 BC, when their civilization ended, trade had spread Olmec **culture**.

> Underline the sentence that tells when the first civilization developed in Mesoamerica.

The Maya civilization followed the Olmec. The Maya built large stone temples, pyramids, and canals that controlled the flow of water through their cities. The Maya civilization began to collapse in the 900s, but historians are still not sure why.

The Aztec were fierce warriors who migrated to south and central Mexico in the mid-1100s. They conquered many towns, built a large empire, and controlled a huge trading network. The Aztec capital, Tenochtitlán (tay-nawch-teet-LAHN), founded in 1325 AD, became the greatest city in the Americas and one of the world's largest cities. The Aztec became rich on trade and tributes paid by conquered people.

> What was the greatest city in the Americas during the height of the Aztec culture?
>
> _____
>
> _____

The Inca began as a small tribe in the Andes Mountains. In the mid-1400s, the Inca began expanding their empire until it included much of the western coast of South America and had more than 12 million people. The Inca people had a strong central government and a network of roads and bridges that connected all parts of the territory.

> What evidence do we have that cultures existed in Mesoamerica before the Aztecs?
>
> _____
>
> _____
>
> _____

CHALLENGE ACTIVITY

Critical Thinking: Evaluate Imagine that you lived in Mesoamerica or South America before the arrival of Europeans. Write a short paragraph describing which of the four civilizations discussed above you would have preferred to live in. Be sure to support your answer.

Copyright © by Holt, Rinehart and Winston. All rights reserved.

The World before the Opening of the Atlantic

Section 2

MAIN IDEAS
1. Several early societies developed in North America long before Europeans explored the continent.
2. Geographic areas influenced Native American cultures.
3. Native American cultures shared beliefs about religion and land ownership.

Key Terms and People

pueblos aboveground houses made of a heavy clay called adobe

kivas underground ceremonial chambers at the center of each Anasazi community

totems ancestor or animal spirits of the Native Americans of the Pacific Northwest

teepees cone-shaped shelters made of animal hides by the nomadic plains people

matrilineal a society that traces ancestry through mothers

Iroquois League an alliance of Native Americans in northeastern North America

Section Summary

EARLY SOCIETIES

The earliest people in North America were hunter-gatherers. By 1500 BC people in the southwestern part of North America had farm cultures and grew maize. The Anasazi used irrigation to increase food production in the dry climate. They lived in pit houses dug into the ground and later began to build **pueblos**. The Anasazi often built complex houses on cliff walls to defend against attacks. They also built **kivas**, sacred areas at the center of the community.

> **How would building on cliff walls provide protection for the Anasazi?**
> _____
> _____
> _____

The Anasazi began abandoning their villages after living in them for hundreds of years. Drought, disease, or raids by other tribes may have caused this move.

> **Why would drought be one of the possible reasons that the Anasazi moved from their homes?**
> _____
> _____
> _____

After 1000 BC several farming societies developed in the eastern part of North America. They built large burial mounds to honor their dead. More than 10,000 mounds have been found in the Ohio River valley alone. The largest city of the mound builders had about 30,000 people.

Copyright © by Holt, Rinehart and Winston. All rights reserved.

Interactive Reader and Study Guide

NATIVE AMERICAN CULTURE AREAS

The culture of Native American people varied depending on geography. In the far north, in present-day Alaska and Canada, Native Americans survived primarily by hunting and fishing, living in small groups. Farther south, along the Pacific Northwest, larger groups thrived on the abundant wildlife. They carved tall poles with **totems**—symbols of animal or ancestor spirits—which had religious and cultural meaning.

Farther south along the Pacific and the Sierra Nevada Mountains, people fished, hunted, gathered plants, and lived in small groups of families. In the drier areas of the southwest, Pueblo groups had to develop agriculture to adapt to the climate. They lived in towns of up to 1000 people. Others, such as the Apache and Navajo, formed nomadic groups that survived by hunting, foraging, or raiding other villages.

Most of the Native Americans of the Great Plains were nomadic hunters. They survived on the abundant wildlife of the grasslands, living in **teepees** made of animal hides. Some Plains groups were farmers, including the Pawnee, who had a **matrilineal** society. In the east, many Native Americans had small villages and lived by farming, hunting, and fishing. The **Iroquois League** was an alliance of many groups that defended one another.

> What was the significance of the characters carved on totem poles?
> _____
> _____
> _____

> Describe the food and shelter of the Native Americans of the Great Plains.
> _____
> _____
> _____

SHARED BELIEFS

Although they had many different cultures, Native Americans shared certain beliefs. Their religions were linked to nature, and they believed that the land was for the use of everyone.

CHALLENGE ACTIVITY

Critical Thinking: Comparing Pick two Native American groups from two different culture areas. Make a chart comparing these two societies.

Copyright © by Holt, Rinehart and Winston. All rights reserved.

The World before the Opening of the Atlantic

Section 3

MAIN IDEAS

1. West Africa developed three great kingdoms that grew wealthy through their control of trade.
2. Slaves became a valuable trade item in West Africa.

Key Terms and People

Berbers North African people who established trade routes through West Africa

Mansa Musa a Muslim king who ruled the Mali Empire at the height of its power and who spread Islamic influence through a large part of West Africa

hajj in Islam, a pilgrimage to the holy city of Mecca

mosques Islamic places of worship

Askia the Great the Muslim ruler who led Songhai to the height of its power

Section Summary

WEST AFRICA'S GREAT KINGDOMS

West African trade routes were originally controlled by the **Berbers**, a people of North Africa. Later, three great kingdoms developed in West Africa by winning control of these trade routes.

The first, Ghana, formed when farmers banded together to protect themselves from herders. They built armies whose superior iron weapons let them take control of the trade in salt and gold. Ghana raised money by forcing traders who passed through its lands to pay taxes. The trade routes brought Ghana in contact with different cultures and beliefs. In the 1060s a Muslim group attacked Ghana, forcing its leaders to convert to Islam. Although Ghana was weakened and eventually fell, the influence of Islam remained strong.

Like Ghana, Mali was located along the upper Niger River. The fertile soil and the control of trade on the river allowed Mali to become rich and powerful. Its most famous ruler was a Muslim king, **Mansa Musa**. Under his leadership Mali grew in wealth and power. Traders came to Timbuktu, an

> What was the main source of the wealth and power of all the West African empires?
>
> _____
> _____
> _____

> What river flowed through both Ghana and Mali?
>
> _____
> _____

Copyright © by Holt, Rinehart and Winston. All rights reserved.

Interactive Reader and Study Guide

important city, to trade for salt, gold, metals, shells, and other goods.

Because he was a devout Muslim, Mansa Musa left Mali on a **hajj**, or a pilgrimage to Mecca. His influence helped bring Islam to a large part of West Africa. In the 1300s Mansa Musa conquered a kingdom called Songhai, whose people also lived along the Niger River. As the Mali empire weakened in the 1400s, Songhai regained independence.

One of the greatest Songhai rulers was Muhammad Ture. He chose a military title, *askia*, and became known as **Askia the Great**. Like Mansa Musa, Askia was a devout Muslim who supported education and learning. His cities had great **mosques**, schools, and libraries. He built a professional army and organized Songhai with governors who were loyal to him. Songhai declined soon after Askia the Great lost power.

> What did Mansa Musa and Askia the Great have in common?
> _____
> _____

WEST AFRICAN SLAVE TRADE

Slavery had existed in Africa and in many parts of the world for centuries. Starting in the 600s Arabs and then Europeans became slave traders. Criminals and people captured during battle could be sold into slavery as well as relatives of people who owed money.

The market for West African slaves increased as Muslim traders took black Africans to sell in North Africa. West Africa was also the home of many slaves taken to the Americas. The slave trade became a key part of the West African economy, contributing to the power of the great empires.

> Underline the sentence that explains how it was determined who would become a slave in West Africa.

CHALLENGE ACTIVITY

Critical Thinking: Elaborate Imagine that you live in one of the kingdoms discussed in this section. Write a brief description of what an average day might be like.

Copyright © by Holt, Rinehart and Winston. All rights reserved.

The World before the Opening of the Atlantic

MAIN IDEAS
1. The Greeks and Romans established new forms of government.
2. During the Middle Ages, society eventually changed from a feudal system to a system with a middle class of artisans and merchants.
3. The Renaissance was a time of rebirth in the arts and in learning.

Key Terms and People

Socrates Greek teacher who wanted people to question their own beliefs

Plato Greek philosopher who wrote *Republic*, about an ideal society

Aristotle Greek philosopher who thought people should live based on reason

reason clear or ordered thinking

democracy a form of government in which people rule themselves

knights feudal warriors who fought on horseback

Black Death a disease that spread across Europe, killing 25 million people

Michelangelo Italian Renaissance artist known for paintings and sculpture

Leonardo da Vinci Italian artist, inventor, engineer, and mapmaker of the Renaissance

Johannes Gutenberg German inventor of the moveable type printing press

joint-stock companies businesses in which a group of people invest together

Academic Vocabulary

classical referring to the cultures of ancient Greece and Rome

Section Summary

GREEK AND ROMAN GOVERNMENT

Ancient Greeks valued human reason and believed in the power of the human mind to think, explain, and understand life. Three of the greatest Greek thinkers were **Socrates**, **Plato**, and **Aristotle**, who were all philosophers and teachers. Aristotle taught that people should live lives based on **reason**, or clear and ordered thinking.

One of the most lasting contributions of the Greeks is their political system. Established during the **Classical** Period, **democracy** is the system in which people rule themselves. Rome later formed a

> Who were three of the greatest Greek thinkers?
> _____
> _____
> _____

> Underline the sentence that describes the Greek contribution of a political system.

Copyright © by Holt, Rinehart and Winston. All rights reserved.

Interactive Reader and Study Guide

Section 4, *continued*

type of democracy called a republic, in which people elect representatives to rule them. These political ideas still influence world governments, including that of the United States.

MIDDLE AGES

After the fall of the Roman empire, Europe was divided into many small kingdoms. A system called feudalism was established in which nobles gave **knights** land in exchange for protection.

In the 1000s important changes began to occur in Europe. The Crusades brought trade with places outside Europe, introducing new products and ideas. Trade also brought a disease known as the **Black Death** that killed much of the population of Europe and caused a shortage of workers. These changes resulted in the development of a middle-class made up of artisans and merchants. Cities became important as commercial centers for trade.

> How did the Black Death cause changes in commerce?
> _____
> _____
> _____

RENAISSANCE

The key feature of the Renaissance was a love of art and education. The search for knowledge spread to all fields. During the Renaissance the focus shifted from religion to people. Two of the great Renaissance artists, **Michelangelo** and **Leonardo da Vinci**, are famous for their paintings, sculpture, and architecture, which reflected the value of the human being. The printing press developed by **Johannes Gutenberg** helped spread new ideas in science, math, and literature.

> Underline the key feature of the Renaissance.

Increased trade caused a commercial revolution. Italian cities became important trading centers. As commerce grew, so did the need for banks. Merchants created **joint-stock companies** in which groups of people invested together.

> What helped spread new ideas during the Renaissance?
> _____
> _____
> _____

CHALLENGE ACTIVITY

Critical Thinking: Evaluate Make a chart showing some of democracy's advantages.

Copyright © by Holt, Rinehart and Winston. All rights reserved.

Interactive Reader and Study Guide

New Empires in the Americas

CHAPTER SUMMARY

CAUSE	EFFECT
Economic growth in Europe	Search for new trade routes to _____ and _____
Search for trade routes	Led to new exchanges between _____, Africa, and the Americas
Need for trading partners by European powers	_____, _____, _____, _____, and _____ established colonies in the Americas.
Death of many Native American people by disease	Shortage of laborers in the colonies led to the development of _____.

COMPREHENSION AND CRITICAL THINKING

As you read the section summaries, fill in the blanks in the graphic organizer above and answer the questions below.

1. Identify Cause and Effect To which continents did Europeans seek new trade routes in the 1400s? What continent unknown to them did they find?

_____

_____

2. Identify Cause and Effect How did the Spanish conquests help Spain grow rich?

_____

_____

3. Make Inferences How do you think the military strength of European countries centuries ago affects cultures in the Americas today?

_____

_____

4. Identify Cause and Effect How did the colonists find forced laborers to replace the Native Americans whose populations were devastated by disease?

_____

_____

Copyright © by Holt, Rinehart and Winston. All rights reserved.

New Empires in the Americas

MAIN IDEAS

1. Vikings were skilled sailors, and they were the first Europeans to reach North America.

2. Prince Henry the Navigator established a school for sailors and provided financial support that enabled the Portuguese to start exploring the oceans.

3. Portuguese sailors sailed around Africa and found a sea route to Asia.

Key Terms and People

Leif Eriksson Viking who landed in present-day Canada in AD1000

Henry the Navigator Portuguese prince who established a school of navigation and paid for expeditions

astrolabe a device used to determine location based on the position of the stars

caravels Portuguese ships that used triangular sails to sail against the wind

Academic Vocabulary

effect the result of an action or decision

Section Summary

VIKING SAILORS REACH NORTH AMERICA

The Vikings were the first Europeans to make contact with North America. They were skilled sailors who developed a new style of ship that was more stable on rough seas.

> Who were the first Europeans to settle in North America?
> _____
> _____

In the year 1000, **Leif Eriksson**, the son of Erik the Red, set off for Greenland. Strong winds blew his ship off course, and he landed on the North American coast. The Vikings settled in a coastal area that Eriksson called Vinland, but they left after a few years. Europeans did not return to the continent for centuries.

PRINCE HENRY THE NAVIGATOR

In the early 1400s Portugal became a leader in world exploration. Although he never set out on a voyage himself, Prince **Henry the Navigator** helped Portugal's explorers succeed. He built an

> What European country led world exploration in the early 1400s?
> _____
> _____

Copyright © by Holt, Rinehart and Winston. All rights reserved.

Interactive Reader and Study Guide

Section 1, *continued*

observatory and a school of navigation to teach better methods of sailing. Europeans had several reasons to explore the world. They wanted spices from
Asia, and they wanted to learn more about Asia and
its culture. They also wanted to convert Asians to
the Christian faith.

> **Why did Europeans want to explore the world?**
> _____
> _____

European sailors were able to travel in open seas
without landmarks to guide them because of new
technology. The **astrolabe** was used to chart a ship's
location based on the position of the stars. The
caravel was a new kind of ship that was smaller,
lighter, and easier to steer. Caravels used triangular
sails that allowed ships to sail against the wind and
rudders that improved steering.

A SEA ROUTE TO ASIA

In the 1400s Portuguese sailors traveled south along
the coast of Africa, setting up trading posts along
the way. In 1497 a Portuguese expedition led by
Vasco da Gama sailed around the southern tip of
Africa and reached India. These successful voyages
had a number of **effects**, both positive and negative.
Portugal's wealth and power increased. However,
these travels eventually led to the spread of the slave
trade. Other European nations soon began looking
for their own sea routes to Asia.

> **What was the first sea route from Europe to Asia?**
> _____
> _____

CHALLENGE ACTIVITY

Critical Thinking: Making Inferences The Portuguese had laws that
included severe penalties for letting sailors from other countries see the
maps the Portuguese created from their expeditions. Write a paragraph
explaining why they wanted to keep these maps secret.

Copyright © by Holt, Rinehart and Winston. All rights reserved.

New Empires in the Americas

MAIN IDEAS

1. Christopher Columbus sailed across the Atlantic Ocean and reached a continent that was previously unknown to him.
2. After Columbus's voyages, other explorers sailed to the Americas.

Key Terms and People

Christopher Columbus a sailor from Genoa, Italy

Line of Demarcation an imaginary boundary in the Atlantic dividing Spanish and Portuguese territories

Treaty of Tordesillas agreement between Spain and Portugal moving the Line of Demarcation

Ferdinand Magellan Portuguese navigator whose expedition circumnavigated the globe

circumnavigate to go all the way around the globe

Columbian Exchange the transfer of plants and animals between the Americas and Asia, Africa, and Europe

Section Summary

COLUMBUS SAILS ACROSS THE ATLANTIC

Christopher Columbus, a sailor from Genoa, Italy, believed that he could reach Asia by sailing west across the Atlantic Ocean. He asked King Ferdinand and Queen Isabella of Spain to pay for an expedition. In return, he promised great riches, new territory, and Catholic converts.

Sailing with three ships, Columbus reached an island in the Bahamas in 1492. Columbus thought he had found a new route to Asia. In reality he had reached another continent that was unknown to him. Columbus made three more journeys to the Americas during his lifetime. When he died in 1506 he still believed that he had reached Asia.

The voyages of Columbus changed the way Europeans saw the world and also created conflict between European nations. In 1493 the pope issued a decree that created the **Line of Demarcation**.

> Why did the Spanish and other Europeans want to find a route to Asia?
>
> _____
>
> _____

> Underline the sentence that explains where Columbus thought he had landed.

Copyright © by Holt, Rinehart and Winston. All rights reserved.

Interactive Reader and Study Guide

Section 2, *continued*

This imaginary boundary divided the Atlantic
Ocean between Spain and Portugal. The Portuguese
king believed the arrangement favored Spain, so
the leaders of the two nations signed the **Treaty
of Tordesillas.** This treaty moved the Line of
Demarcation 800 miles further west and prevented
a war between the two countries.

> **What was the purpose of the Treaty of Tordesillas?**
> _____
> _____
> _____

OTHER EXPLORERS SAIL TO THE AMERICAS

After Columbus other explorers sailed across the
Atlantic Ocean. In 1501 Amerigo Vespucci became
convinced that he had not reached Asia but had
discovered a "new world." A German mapmaker
labeled the continents across the ocean as *America*
in his honor.

Vasco Núñez de Balboa, a Spanish explorer,
crossed the jungles of Central America to see the
Pacific Ocean in 1513. In 1519 Portuguese navigator **Ferdinand Magellan** sailed around the southern
tip of South America and into the Pacific. Although
Magellan was killed in the Philippine Islands, one
ship from his expedition was the first to **circumnavigate,** or go all the way around, the globe.

> **Why do people say that Ferdinand Magellan circumnavigated the globe even though he died on the way?**
> _____
> _____
> _____

European explorers and settlers took plants and
animals with them to America and brought back
American plants and animals. This transfer was
called the **Columbian Exchange** because it started
with the explorations of Columbus. Over time a
trading pattern developed, involving the exchange
of raw materials, manufactured products, and slaves
among Europe, Africa, and the Americas.

CHALLENGE ACTIVITY

Critical Thinking: Elaborating Imagine you are a sailor on one of
Columbus's ships. Write a short poem about the first sighting of land in
the present-day Bahamas.

Copyright © by Holt, Rinehart and Winston. All rights reserved.

New Empires in the Americas

> **MAIN IDEAS**
> 1. Spanish conquistadors conquered the Aztec and Inca empires.
> 2. Spanish explorers traveled through the borderlands of New Spain, claiming more land.
> 3. Spanish settlers treated Native Americans harshly, forcing them to work on plantations and in mines.

Key Terms and People

conquistadors Spanish soldiers who led military expeditions in the Americas

Hernán Cortés conquistador who conquered the Aztec empire

Moctezuma II ruler of the Aztec empire

Francisco Pizarro a conquistador who captured the Inca capital and killed the Inca leaders

encomienda system a system that gave settlers the right to tax Native Americans or to make them work

plantations large farms that grew just one kind of crop and made huge profits for their owners

Bartolomé de Las Casas a priest who encouraged better treatment of Native Americans

Section Summary

SPANISH CONQUISTADORS

The Spanish sent **conquistadors** to the Americas on military expeditions. Conquistador **Hernán Cortés** went to present-day Mexico in 1519. He had heard of land to the west ruled by **Moctezuma II**, the king of the Aztec empire. The Spaniards believed the Aztec lands were a rich source of gold and silver. They also wanted to convert the Aztec to Christianity.

Although they were greatly outnumbered, the conquistadors had superior weapons and formed alliances with enemies of the Aztec. Cortés took control of the Aztec capital and killed Moctezuma. Smallpox and other European diseases sped up the fall of the Aztec empire.

> **Why might Cortés have wanted to conquer the Aztec?**
> _____
> _____
> _____

> **What advantage did the Spanish have over the Aztec?**
> _____
> _____
> _____

Copyright © by Holt, Rinehart and Winston. All rights reserved.

Interactive Reader and Study Guide

While seeking gold **Francisco Pizarro** led his troops to capture the great Inca capital at Cuzco. Within a few years Pizarro had conquered the entire Inca empire. The Spanish then began to create a vast empire which they called New Spain. They established settlements to serve as trading posts, missions to convert local Native Americans to Catholicism, and military bases.

> **Why did Pizarro first enter the Inca empire?**
> _____
> _____

EXPLORING THE BORDERLANDS OF NEW SPAIN

Spain's empire in America extended well beyond the lands taken from the Aztec and Inca. Regions claimed by the Spanish explorers included the island of Puerto Rico, the coast of present-day Florida, and the coastal regions of the Gulf of Mexico. The Spanish also explored what is now the southwestern United States, looking for cities of gold that were rumored to exist there. They traveled through unclaimed areas of Texas, Oklahoma, and as far north as Kansas.

SPANISH TREATMENT OF NATIVE AMERICANS

California was among the last borderlands settled by the Spanish. To pay back settlers for their work, Spain established the **encomienda system**. It gave settlers the right to tax Native Americans and make them work. Most of the workers were treated as slaves and forced to work on **plantations** in New Spain. Many Native Americans died of disease and exhaustion. The priest **Bartolomé de Las Casas** spoke out against the terrible treatment of Native Americans.

> **Why might de Las Casas have spoken out against the encomienda system?**
> _____
> _____

CHALLENGE ACTIVITY

Critical Thinking: Identifying Cause and Effect Make a chart showing the causes and effects of Spain's conquests in the Americas.

Copyright © by Holt, Rinehart and Winston. All rights reserved.

Interactive Reader and Study Guide

Name _____ Class _____ Date _____

New Empires in the Americas

MAIN IDEAS

1. Events in Europe affected settlement of North America.
2. Several explorers searched for a Northwest Passage to the Pacific Ocean.
3. European nations raced to establish empires in North America.

Key Terms and People

Protestant Reformation a religious movement that began as an effort to reform the Catholic Church

Protestants the reformers who protested the Catholic Church's practices

Spanish Armada the Spanish fleet of huge warships

Northwest Passage a path through North America that would allow ships to sail from the Atlantic to the Pacific

Jacques Cartier French explorer who sailed up the Saint Lawrence River looking for the Northwest Passage

charter a document giving permission to start a colony

Section Summary

EVENTS IN EUROPE

In 1517 a priest named Martin Luther launched the **Protestant Reformation**. His followers were called **Protestants**. Luther said the Catholic Church was too rich and abused its powers. The printing press helped spread Protestant ideas because large numbers of Bibles could be printed. More people could read the Bible on their own instead of depending on priests to explain it.

> **How did the printing press help spread Protestant ideas?**
> _____
> _____

Often conflicts between Catholics and Protestants led to war. In the late 1500s French Catholics fought French Protestants known as Huguenots. Many Huguenots traveled to the Americas for religious freedom. In 1534 King Henry VIII established the Church of England, or Anglican Church. Henry declared himself head of this Protestant church. By breaking with the Catholic church, King Henry made himself the enemy of other European rulers who were Catholics.

> **What were French Protestants called?**
> _____
> _____

Copyright © by Holt, Rinehart and Winston. All rights reserved.

Interactive Reader and Study Guide

King Philip II of Spain, a Catholic ruler, put together a large fleet called the **Spanish Armada** to defeat the Protestant nation of England. England had fewer ships, but they were quick. In July 1588 the English navy defeated the Armada. The defeat hurt the Spanish, whose economy was in trouble because of inflation. Inflation is a rise in prices caused by an increase in the amount of money in use.

> **What helped England's navy defeat the Spanish Armada?**
> _____
> _____

SEARCH FOR A NORTHWEST PASSAGE

European nations wanted to find a **Northwest Passage** in North America that would allow ships to sail from the Atlantic to the Pacific. Early searches explored the coast from Canada to North Carolina. **Jacques Cartier** explored the Saint Lawrence River and claimed lands for France. The Northwest Passage was not found, but the voyages led to more interest in North America.

EUROPEAN PRESENCE IN NORTH AMERICA

Spain and Portugal claimed much of South and Central America but left most of North America unexplored. In the late 1500s Sir Walter Raleigh of England received a **charter** to found a colony in present-day Virginia. The first colonists did not stay, but Raleigh sent more colonists. Those colonists disappeared.

France built settlements in Florida, but the Spanish soon drove them out. In the 1600s French colonies were established on the Saint Lawrence River. The French claimed lands extending to the Mississippi River. The Dutch founded the town of New Amsterdam on Manhattan Island. Swedish settlers started New Sweden along the Delaware River, but it was conquered by the Dutch colonists in 1655.

> **What happened to French settlers in Florida?**
> _____
> _____

CHALLENGE ACTIVITY

Critical Thinking: Summarizing Write a bulleted list summarizing the early settlements of the Americas.

Copyright © by Holt, Rinehart and Winston. All rights reserved.

Interactive Reader and Study Guide

New Empires in the Americas

MAIN IDEAS

1. European diseases wiped out much of the Native American population, causing colonists to look for a new labor force.
2. Europeans enslaved millions of Africans and sent them to work in their colonies.
3. Slaves in the Americas created a distinct culture.

Key Terms and People

immune having a natural resistance to a disease

Middle Passage the voyage across the Atlantic that enslaved Africans were forced to endure

African Diaspora the scattering of African people due to slavery

Academic Vocabulary

structure the way something is organized

Section Summary

THE NEED FOR A NEW LABOR FORCE

Diseases like measles, smallpox, and typhus had afflicted Europeans for many centuries. As a result, Europeans were more **immune** to the diseases. Native Americans were not. Therefore, these European diseases had a devastating effect on the Native American population.

Now the European colonists needed a new workforce for their plantations. Plantations were important to the colonial economic **structure**. As Africans had already developed some immunity to European diseases, the colonists decided that slaves from West Africa could be the solution to the labor problem.

> How did the lack of immunity to disease affect the Native American peoples?
>
> _____
>
> _____

> What factors caused colonists to decide to use African slaves?
>
> _____
>
> _____
>
> _____

THE SLAVE TRADE

In 1510 the Spanish government legalized the sale of slaves in its colonies. Over the next century, more than a million African slaves were brought to the Spanish and Portugese colonies. The English and Dutch were also active slave traders.

Copyright © by Holt, Rinehart and Winston. All rights reserved.

Section 5, continued

Enslaved people were often captured in the interior of Africa, chained, and forced to march up to 1,000 miles to the coast. They were then chained together and packed as cargo in the lower decks of ships crossing the Atlantic Ocean. This voyage was known as the **Middle Passage**. In the crowded ships, disease spread quickly. Many of the slaves died of sickness, suffocation, or malnutrition during the voyage.

Between the 1520s and the 1860s, about 12 million Africans were shipped across the Atlantic as slaves. The slave trade led to the **African Diaspora**. Slaves had few rights in the colonies and were considered to be property. The treatment of enslaved Africans varied, but severe treatment and dreadful punishments were often part of American slavery.

> How many people were shipped from Africa as part of the slave trade?
> _____

SLAVE CULTURE IN THE AMERICAS

Slaves in America came from many parts of Africa. They spoke different languages and had different cultural backgrounds, but they also shared many customs and viewpoints. They built a new culture on the things they had in common.

Families were a key part of slave culture, but slave families faced many challenges. A family was often broken apart when members were sold to different owners. Religion was a refuge for slaves. Slave religion was primarily Christian, but it also included traditional elements from African religions. Religion gave slaves a sense of self worth and hope for salvation. Slaves used songs and folktales to tell stories of sorrow, hope, agony, and joy.

> Underline the sentence that describes the kind of religion that was common among slaves in the Americas.

CHALLENGE ACTIVITY

Critical Thinking: Elaborate Write a song or folktale that reflects the experiences of enslaved Africans. Your song or folktale should reflect the feelings of sorrow, hope, agony and joy that were included in the songs and folktales of slaves.

Copyright © by Holt, Rinehart and Winston. All rights reserved.

Interactive Reader and Study Guide

The English Colonies

CHAPTER SUMMARY

Southern Colonies	New England Colonies	Middle Colonies
Farming	_____ _____	Trade and staple crops
_____ _____	Religion linked to government	Religious tolerance
_____ _____	Difficult start, soon prospered	_____ _____

COMPREHENSION AND CRITICAL THINKING

As you read the section summaries, fill in the blanks in the graphic organizer above and answer the questions below.

1. Classify Which colonies had difficulty in the beginning but soon flourished? Which colonies prospered from the start?

_____

_____

2. Classify Which colonies relied on trade? In which was farming important?

_____

_____

3. Compare and Contrast Compare and contrast religion in the three regions.

_____

_____

_____

_____

_____

_____

Copyright © by Holt, Rinehart and Winston. All rights reserved.

The English Colonies

MAIN IDEAS

1. Jamestown was the first permanent English settlement in America.
2. Daily life in Virginia was challenging to the colonists.
3. Religious freedom and economic opportunities were motives for founding other southern colonies, including Maryland, the Carolinas, and Georgia.
4. Farming and slavery were important to the economies of the southern colonies.

Key Terms and People

Jamestown an English settlement in Virginia founded in 1607

John Smith a colonist and leader of Jamestown

Pocahontas a Powhatan Indian who married Jamestown colonist John Rolfe

indentured servants colonists who reached America by working for free for other people who had paid for their journeys

Bacon's Rebellion an uprising led by Nathaniel Bacon against high taxes

Toleration Act of 1649 an act that made limiting the religious rights of Christians a crime

Olaudah Equiano a former slave who wrote down his experiences

slave codes laws to control slaves

Academic Vocabulary

authority power, right to rule

factors causes

Section Summary

SETTLEMENT IN JAMESTOWN

Life in **Jamestown** was hard. Few colonists knew how to grow crops for food. Captain **John Smith** worried about this. Many colonists starved. The Powhatan helped the colonists learn to grow crops.

    Pocahontas helped unite the Powhatan and the colonists, but she died in 1617. Fighting broke out between the colonists and the Powhatan and went on for the next 20 years. The colony existed under the **authority** of a governor chosen by the king.

> Why did many colonists in Jamestown starve?
> _____
> _____

Copyright © by Holt, Rinehart and Winston. All rights reserved.

DAILY LIFE IN VIRGINIA

Colonists began forming large farms called plantations. At first **indentured servants** worked on plantations. Soon the demand for labor began to exceed
the supply. Then in 1619 the first Africans were
brought to Virginia. These **factors** led wealthy
farmers to begin using slave labor.

In 1676 Nathaniel Bacon, a wealthy frontier farmer, led **Bacon's Rebellion**. Bacon and his followers
burned Jamestown.

> What happened to Jamestown in 1676?
> _____
> _____

OTHER SOUTHERN COLONIES

Maryland was founded north of Virginia as a new
colony for Catholics. In the 1640s Protestants began
moving in. Religious problems divided Protestants
and Catholics. The **Toleration Act of 1649** made
limiting religious rights of Christians a crime in
Maryland.

> Circle the sentence that explains what the Toleration Act of 1649 did.

The Carolinas and Georgia were formed south of
Virginia and Maryland. South Carolina had many
large plantations, and owners bought slaves to work
on them. In Georgia many huge rice plantations
were worked by thousands of slaves.

ECONOMIES OF THE SOUTHERN COLONIES

The economies of the southern colonies were
based on farming. Many small farms and some
small plantations meant a large group of workers
was needed. African slaves became these workers.
Slavery was brutal. A former slave named **Olaudah
Equiano** wrote that slaves were often tortured,
murdered, and treated with barbarity. Most of the
southern states passed **slave codes** to control slaves.

> How did a former slave describe treatment of slaves?
> _____
> _____

CHALLENGE ACTIVITY

Critical Thinking: Designing Design a time line showing the dates of
important events in the colonies.

Copyright © by Holt, Rinehart and Winston. All rights reserved.

The English Colonies

MAIN IDEAS

1. The Pilgrims and Puritans came to America to avoid religious persecution.
2. Religion and government were closely linked in the New England colonies.
3. The New England economy was based on trade and farming.
4. Education was important in the New England colonies.

Key Terms and People

Puritans a Protestant group that wanted to reform, or purify, the Church of England

Pilgrims a Protestant group that cut all ties with the Church of England and was punished

immigrants people who have left the country of their birth to live in another country

Mayflower Compact a legal contract male passengers on the Mayflower signed agreeing to have fair laws to protect the general good

Squanto a Patuxet Indian who had lived in Europe and spoke English

John Winthrop the leader of Puritans who left England for Massachusetts seeking religious freedom

Anne Hutchinson a Puritan who claimed to receive her religious views directly from God and who was forced to leave the Massachusetts Bay Colony

Section Summary

PILGRIMS AND PURITANS

The **Pilgrims** were a group of **Puritans** who suffered persecution in England. They became **immigrants**, first settling in the Netherlands and then sailing to America.

When they reached America, the Pilgrims signed the **Mayflower Compact**. This was one of the first times English colonists tried to govern themselves. Earlier, in 1215, English nobles had forced the king to give them some rights in Magna Carta. Later the English Bill of Rights provided more liberties.

The Pilgrims learned to fertilize their soil from **Squanto**. They invited him and 90 Wampanoag guests to a feast now known as Thanksgiving.

Religion and education played important parts in the Pilgrims' lives, which centered on families.

Name two early examples of the English receiving rights.

_____

_____

Copyright © by Holt, Rinehart and Winston. All rights reserved.

Everyone worked hard. Women had rights that they did not have in England.

Puritans and merchants founded the Massachusetts Bay colony. Tens of thousands of English men, women and children would immigrate to it. **John Winthrop** led one group. Puritans believed they had a sacred agreement with God to build a Christian colony.

> **What was the Puritans' sacred agreement with God?**
> _____
> _____

RELIGION AND GOVERNMENT IN NEW ENGLAND

Politics and religion were closely linked in Puritan New England. Some self-government existed. However, only the chosen male church members could vote.

> **Underline the sentence that means women could not vote in Puritan New England.**

Some Puritans had different religious views than others. Minister Roger Williams supported the separation of the church from politics. He founded Providence. **Anne Hutchinson** was forced to leave the colony because of her religious ideas.

NEW ENGLAND ECONOMY

The New England colonies had a hard climate and rocky soil. The kind of farming done in Virginia was impossible there. Instead, they traded goods, fished, built ships, and became skilled craftspeople.

> **Compare sources of income in Virginia and New England.**
> _____
> _____

EDUCATION IN THE COLONIES

New England parents wanted their children to read the Bible. They made laws requiring the education of children. The colonists also founded Harvard College to teach ministers.

CHALLENGE ACTIVITY

Critical Thinking: Developing Questions Develop three questions about the Pilgrims' contributions and research to answer them.

Copyright © by Holt, Rinehart and Winston. All rights reserved.

The English Colonies

> **MAIN IDEAS**
> 1. The English created New York and New Jersey from former Dutch territory.
> 2. William Penn established the colony of Pennsylvania.
> 3. The economy of the middle colonies was supported by trade and staple crops.

Key Terms and People

Peter Stuyvesant director general who took control of New Amsterdam beginning in 1647

Quakers a Protestant religious group founded by George Fox in the mid-1600s in England

William Penn a Quaker leader who began the Pennsylvania colony

staple crops crops that are always needed, such as wheat, barley, and oats

Section Summary

NEW YORK AND NEW JERSEY

In 1613 the Dutch formed New Netherland as a base for trading fur with the Iroquois. They traded fur mostly in the town of New Amsterdam on Manhattan Island. Large land grants and religious tolerance meant Jews, French Huguenots, Puritans, and others came to the colony.

> What was the first name of New York City?
>
> _____
> _____

Peter Stuyvesant ruled the colony for many years. Then in 1664 an English fleet gained control of New Netherland without any fighting. New Amsterdam became New York City, named in honor of the Duke of York. New York was the first of the middle colonies.

> Why did the Dutch settle New Amsterdam?
>
> _____
> _____

The Duke of York made two men proprietors, or governors, of New Jersey. The colony rested between the Hudson and Delaware Rivers. Dutch, Finns, Swedes, Scots, and others lived there.

> Underline the sentence that makes you think the population of New Jersey was diverse.

PENN'S COLONY

One of the biggest religious groups in New Jersey was the Society of Friends, or the **Quakers**. Their

Copyright © by Holt, Rinehart and Winston. All rights reserved.

religious practices were different. They believed in the equality of men and women before God. They also backed religious tolerance for all groups. The Quakers' beliefs angered many. They were treated badly in both England and America.

William Penn started a colony named Pennsylvania. He offered religious freedom to all Christians. He created a way to change colony laws based on what the people wanted. Many Quakers settled in Pennsylvania. Penn named his capital Philadelphia, which means "the city of Brotherly Love."

> **What does Philadelphia mean?**
> _____
> _____

ECONOMY OF THE MIDDLE COLONIES

A good climate and fertile land meant the colonists could grow a large quantity of **staple crops**, unlike colonists in New England. Some slaves worked in the middle colonies but not as many as in the south. Indentured servants did more of the labor.

> **How did the middle and southern colonies differ?**
> _____
> _____

By the 1700s Philadelphia and New York City had grown into large cities. Trade was important to the middle colonies. Women ran some businesses and practiced as doctors, nurses, or midwives.

CHALLENGE ACTIVITY

Critical Thinking: Evaluating Think about the two colonies. How are they similar? How are they different? Decide which colony you would like to live in. Then write a short essay explaining why you chose the colony you did. Illustrate your essay.

Copyright © by Holt, Rinehart and Winston. All rights reserved.

The English Colonies

MAIN IDEAS

1. Colonial governments were influenced by political changes in England.
2. English trade laws limited free trade in the colonies.
3. The Great Awakening and the Enlightenment led to ideas of political equality among many colonists.
4. The French and Indian War gave England control of more land in North America.

Key Terms and People

town meeting an assembly in which colonists decided issues and made laws

English Bill of Rights an act passed in 1689 that reduced the powers of the English monarch and gave Parliament more power

triangular trade indirect trade between the American colonies and Britain

Jonathan Edwards important leader of the Great Awakening

Great Awakening an awakening in the religious lives of colonists

Enlightenment a movement during the 1700s that focused on the use of reason and logic to improve society

Pontiac Native American leader who led a rebellion in the Ohio Valley in 1763

Section Summary

COLONIAL GOVERNMENTS

The House of Burgesses helped make laws in Virginia. In New England, colonists at **town meeting** decided local issues. The middle colonies used both county courts and town meetings.

King James II of England thought the colonies were too independent. He united the northern colonies and limited their powers. In 1689 the **English Bill of Rights** shifted power from the monarch to Parliament, the British governing body. These rights were not extended to the colonists.

> How were laws made in Virginia and New England?
>
> _____
> _____

> Did the colonists benefit from the English Bill of Rights?
>
> _____
> _____

ENGLISH TRADE LAWS

England controlled its American colonies partly to earn money. Parliament passed Navigation Acts that required colonists to trade only with Britain.

Copyright © by Holt, Rinehart and Winston. All rights reserved.

However, some colonists wanted to buy and sell goods at the market offering the best prices.

In a deadly version of **triangular trade**, New England colonists traded rum for slaves from the African coast. The slave trade forced 10 million Africans across the Atlantic Ocean. In the Middle Passage thousands of them died.

> What is the name given to the voyage of slaves from Africa to America?
>
> _____

GREAT AWAKENING AND ENLIGHTENMENT

During the **Great Awakening** talk of spiritual equality made some people, such as **Jonathan Edwards**, think about political equality. **Enlightenment** thinker John Locke said people should obey their rulers only if the state protected life, liberty, and property.

In 1675 a war erupted between New England colonists and some American Indians. Metacomet, who was also known as King Philip, led the Wampanoag. Each side killed men, women, and children. The fighting ended in 1676.

> What was King Philip's real name?
>
> _____

FRENCH AND INDIAN WAR

The British and the French both wanted to control certain territory in North America. The French and Indian War was about the British wanting to settle in the Ohio Valley and the French wanting it for the fur trade. After the war Britain won Canada and all French lands east of the Mississippi River.

The Ohio Valley proved good for farming, but Native American leaders opposed British settlements. American Indian Chief **Pontiac** led followers against the British. He later gave up, but King George III banned colonists from settling on Indian lands. Many settlers ignored the ban.

> How did many Americans react to the king's ban on settling on Indian lands?

CHALLENGE ACTIVITY

Critical Thinking: Drawing Inferences Imagine you live during the Enlightenment. Write a short journal entry describing the time.

Copyright © by Holt, Rinehart and Winston. All rights reserved.

The English Colonies

MAIN IDEAS

1. British efforts to raise taxes on colonists sparked protest.
2. The Boston Massacre caused colonial resentment toward Great Britain.
3. Colonists protested the British tax on tea with the Boston Tea Party.
4. Great Britain responded to colonial actions by passing the Intolerable Acts.

Key Terms and People

Samuel Adams Boston leader who believed Parliament could not tax the colonists without their permission

Committees of Correspondence method of communication between towns and colonies about British laws

Stamp Act of 1765 required colonists to pay for an official stamp when buying paper items

Boston Massacre shooting by British soldiers killed five colonists

Tea Act an act allowing a British company to sell cheap tea directly to the colonists

Boston Tea Party a protest in which colonists dressed as American Indians and dumped 340 tea chests from British ships into Boston Harbor

Intolerable Acts laws passed to punish colonists for the Boston Tea Party

Section Summary

GREAT BRITAIN RAISES TAXES

Parliament raised the colonists' taxes for money to pay for the French and Indian War. The tax money was also used to keep a British army in North America to protect the colonists against American Indian attacks. Parliament also tried harder to arrest smugglers avoiding taxes.

Many colonists believed Britain had no right to tax them without their permission. Colonists communicated their ideas about British laws in **Committees of Correspondence. Samuel Adams** and James Otis spread the slogan "No Taxation without Representation." Colonists chose to boycott, refusing to buy British goods. They hoped

Name one reason that Parliament raised taxes.

_____

_____

How did colonists respond to British taxes?

_____

_____

Copyright © by Holt, Rinehart and Winston. All rights reserved.

Parliament would end the new taxes. The **Stamp Act of 1765** meant a tax had to be paid on legal documents, licenses, and other items.

The Townshend Acts charged taxes on imported glass, lead, paints, paper, and tea. Boston's Sons of Liberty attacked the customs houses to protest the taking of a ship on suspicion of smuggling. British soldiers came in 1768 to restore order.

> **Underline the sentence that tells what the Townshend Acts did.**

BOSTON MASSACRE

On March 5, 1770, a few troops fired on Bostonians who were throwing snowballs at them. That led to the **Boston Massacre**. The soldiers and their officer were charged with murder. A jury found the officer and six soldiers acted in self-defense and were not guilty. Two soldiers were convicted of accidental killing. This calmed Boston for a while.

> **Why do you think the jury found some of the troops not guilty?**
> _____
> _____
> _____

THE BOSTON TEA PARTY

Parliament ended almost all the Townshend Acts but left the tax on tea. Colonists united against the **Tea Act**. In November 1773 the **Boston Tea Party** showed the colonists' spirit of rebellion.

THE INTOLERABLE ACTS

The Boston Tea Party made the new British Prime Minister very angry. Parliament punished Boston by passing the **Intolerable Acts**. The laws closed Boston Harbor until the colonists paid for the lost tea. Other parts of the Intolerable Acts angered the colonists even more.

> **Why did the Boston Tea Party anger the British Prime Minister?**
> _____
> _____
> _____

CHALLENGE ACTIVITY

Critical Thinking: Imagining Imagine you write for Boston's Committee of Correspondence. Give a brief description of the Boston Massacre.

Copyright © by Holt, Rinehart and Winston. All rights reserved.

The American Revolution

CHAPTER SUMMARY

Declaration of Rights	led to	"Shot heard 'round the world"
Declaration of Independence	led to	Break with Britain
Battle of Saratoga	led to	
Battle of Yorktown	led to	

COMPREHENSION AND CRITICAL THINKING

As you read the section summaries, fill in the table above and answer
the questions below.

1. Recall Which battle was the turning point of the Revolutionary War?

_____

_____

2. Identify Cause and Effect Which battle led to the victory of the Patriot forces in
the Revolutionary War?

_____

_____

3. Evaluate Do you think the Patriots could have won the Revolutionary War without help from other countries? Why or why not?

_____

_____

4. Make Judgments Do you think it was better to fight the British than to continue
working toward a peaceful solution? Why or why not?

_____

_____

Copyright © by Holt, Rinehart and Winston. All rights reserved.

The American Revolution

MAIN IDEAS

1. The First Continental Congress demanded certain rights from Great Britain.

2. Armed conflict between British soldiers and colonists broke out with the "shot heard 'round the world."

3. The Second Continental Congress created the Continental Army to fight the British.

4. In two early battles, the army lost control of Boston but then regained it.

Key Terms and People

First Continental Congress gathering of colonial leaders who were deeply troubled about the relationship between Great Britain and its colonies in America

Patriots colonists who chose to fight for independence

minutemen the members of the civilian volunteer militia

Redcoats British soldiers wearing red uniforms

Second Continental Congress meeting of delegates from 12 colonies in Philadelphia in May 1775

Continental Army army created by the Second Continental Congress to carry out the fight against Britain

George Washington the Virginian who commanded the Continental Army

Battle of Bunker Hill battle won by the British but with double the American losses

Academic Vocabulary

reaction response

Section Summary

FIRST CONTINENTAL CONGRESS

Delegates to the **First Continental Congress** were worried about the relationship between Great Britain and its American colonies. The delegates debated whether violence was avoidable. They encouraged the peaceful boycott of British goods but also began preparing for war. They drafted a Declaration of Rights, but King George refused to consider it. Colonists who chose to fight for independence were known as **Patriots**.

What did the delegates debate?

_____

_____

Copyright © by Holt, Rinehart and Winston. All rights reserved.

Section 1, continued

"SHOT HEARD 'ROUND THE WORLD"

On April 19, 1775, 700 **Redcoats** set out for
Concord. A British general sent the soldiers to
destroy a weapons storehouse they thought was
there. Three colonists rode out on horseback to
warn that the British were coming. Seventy armed
minutemen waited for the British at Lexington. To
this day nobody knows who fired the first shot. The
British killed eight minutemen, then went on to
Concord where they destroyed a few buildings. In
reaction the minutemen fired on the Redcoats. The
British suffered many casualties and were forced to
retreat.

> Why did the British soldiers go to Concord?
> _____
> _____

SECOND CONTINENTAL CONGRESS

At the **Second Continental Congress** some del-
egates called for war while others wanted peace.
The Congress named the Massachusetts militia the
Continental Army. The army's commander was
George Washington. Delegates signed the Olive
Branch Petition asking King George to make peace.
He would not consider it.

> What was King George's response to the Olive Branch Petition?
> _____
> _____

EARLY BATTLES

On June 17, 1775, the British in Boston found colonial forces dug in on Breed's Hill. When the British
crossed the harbor in boats to take the hill, the colonists opened fire. The British took the hill on their
third try. But the **Battle of Bunker Hill** proved the
colonists could hold their own. Soon after, General
Washington took command of the Continental
Army in Boston. He set up cannons from Fort
Ticonderoga to fire on the British. On March 7,
1776, the British retreated from Boston.

CHALLENGE ACTIVITY

Critical Thinking: Analyze List several rights we have as U.S. citizens.

Copyright © by Holt, Rinehart and Winston. All rights reserved.

Interactive Reader and Study Guide

The American Revolution

MAIN IDEAS

1. Thomas Paine's *Common Sense* led many colonists to support independence.
2. Colonists had to choose sides when independence was declared.
3. The Declaration of Independence did not address the rights of all colonists.

Key Terms and People

Common Sense a 47-page pamphlet that argued against British rule over America

Thomas Paine author of *Common Sense*, who wrote that citizens, not monarchs, should make laws

Thomas Jefferson the main author of the Declaration of Independence

Declaration of Independence the document that formally announced the colonies' break from Great Britain

Loyalists colonists, sometimes called Tories, who remained loyal to Britain

Section Summary

PAINE'S *COMMON SENSE*

Common Sense was published anonymously, or without the name of its author, who was **Thomas Paine**. At this time the idea that citizens should pass laws made news. As word of the pamphlet spread throughout the colonies, it eventually sold about 500,000 copies. The pamphlet made a strong case for political and economic freedom. It supported the right to military self-defense. *Common Sense* changed the way many colonists viewed their king.

> Why do you think *Common Sense* was so popular?
> _____
> _____

INDEPENDENCE IS DECLARED

The first point argued by **Thomas Jefferson** in the **Declaration of Independence** was that all men possess unalienable rights, or rights that cannot be denied. These rights include "life, liberty, and the pursuit of happiness." Jefferson also maintained that King George III had trampled on the colonists' rights by supporting unfair laws and wrongly meddling in colonial governments. In addition Jefferson argued that the colonies had the right

Copyright © by Holt, Rinehart and Winston. All rights reserved.

Interactive Reader and Study Guide

Section 2, *continued*

to independence from Britain. He believed in the Enlightenment idea of the social contract. This idea says that citizens should agree to be governed only when rulers and governments support their rights. Jefferson said that King George III had violated the social contract, so the colonies should not obey his laws.

> **Why did Jefferson think the colonies should not obey King George III?**
> _____
> _____

On July 4, 1776, the Continental Congress voted in favor of the Declaration of Independence. In approving the Declaration, the Congress finally broke away from Great Britain. Today we celebrate the Fourth of July as the birthday of our nation.

Not everyone rejoiced over the approval of the Declaration. Patriots and **Loyalists** became divided. Sometimes family members were on opposite sides during the war. More than 50,000 Loyalists left the colonies during the Revolution.

> **What did some families experience during the war?**
> _____
> _____

UNFINISHED BUSINESS

Looking back, we realize that the Declaration paid no attention to many colonists. Abigail Adams, wife of delegate John Adams, tried to influence him to include women in the Declaration. It did not happen. Enslaved African Americans also had no rights under the Declaration. Slavery was legal in all colonies in July 1776. The Revolutionary War would not end the battle over slavery, even though New England states moved to end it by the 1780s.

> **Name two groups who had no rights under the Declaration.**
> _____
> _____

CHALLENGE ACTIVITY

Critical Thinking: Develop Imagine that you are a delegate to the Second Continental Congress. Deliver a two-minute speech arguing that the Declaration should also give women and slaves rights.

Copyright © by Holt, Rinehart and Winston. All rights reserved.

Interactive Reader and Study Guide

The American Revolution

MAIN IDEAS

1. Many Americans supported the war effort.
2. The Patriots both won and lost battles during the years 1775–1777.
3. France and Spain helped the Patriots fight the British.
4. The winter at Valley Forge tested the strength of Patriot troops.
5. The war continued at sea and in the West.

Key Terms and People

mercenaries foreign soldiers who fought not out of loyalty, but for pay

Battle of Trenton a battle won by the Patriots against mercenary Hessians

Battle of Saratoga a great victory for the American forces in which British General John Burgoyne surrendered his entire army to American General Horatio Gates

Marquis de Lafayette a Frenchman who volunteered to serve in the Continental Army without pay and used his money and influence to support the Patriots

Baron Friedrich von Steuben a Prussian military officer who trained the Continental Army

Bernardo de Gálvez the governor of Spanish Louisiana, who became a Patriot ally

John Paul Jones a brave and clever naval commander

George Rogers Clark a surveyor who led the Patriots' western campaign

Academic Vocabulary

strategy a plan for fighting a battle or war

Section Summary

SUPPORTING THE WAR EFFORT

Life in the army was hard, but the Patriots knew they were fighting for an important cause. More than 230,000 mostly young men served in the Continental Army. After the British promised to free any slaves who fought for them, the Continental Army allowed free African Americans to serve. Women played an important role in the war by helping to supply the army and serving as messengers, nurses, and spies.

> Underline the sentence that tells how some women served the war effort.

Copyright © by Holt, Rinehart and Winston. All rights reserved.

DEFEATS AND VICTORIES

At first the Continental Army lost several battles.
Then the Patriots won an important victory.
British General Howe, who thought the rebellion
would soon be over, left New Jersey in the hands
of Hessian **mercenaries.** The Patriots surprised the
Hessians and won the **Battle of Trenton.**

British General John Burgoyne planned to cut off
New England from the other colonies. His **strategy**
required perfect timing. The Patriots surrounded
Burgoyne and won the **Battle of Saratoga,** which
was the turning point of the war.

> Circle the name of an early victory for the Patriots.

HELP FROM EUROPE

Britain's enemies, France and Spain, began to help
the Patriots. Holland also helped the Patriots.
The **Marquis de Lafayette, Baron Friedrich von
Steuben,** and **Bernardo de Gálvez** joined the war
on the Patriots' side.

WINTER AT VALLEY FORGE

The winter of 1777 turned brutally cold and snowy.
General Washington settled his troops at Valley
Forge, where they bore hardships with courage and
drilled to become better soldiers.

WAR AT SEA AND IN THE WEST

The small Continental Navy sunk hundreds of
British ships. **John Paul Jones** fought a battle with
the British in which his ship took heavy damage.
He fought on, and the British ship surrendered. In
the West, **George Rogers Clark** led Patriots against
British trading villages and Fort Sackville. Clark's
campaigns hurt British support in the West.

> What effect did Clark's campaigns have on the British?
>
> _____
> _____

CHALLENGE ACTIVITY

Critical Thinking: Elaborate Write and perform a dialogue between two
soldiers discussing their hard times at Valley Forge.

Copyright © by Holt, Rinehart and Winston. All rights reserved.

Interactive Reader and Study Guide

The American Revolution

MAIN IDEAS

1. Patriot forces faced many problems in the war in the South.
2. The American Patriots finally defeated the British at the Battle of Yorktown.
3. The British and the Americans officially ended the war by signing the Treaty of Paris of 1783.

Key Terms and People

Francis Marion a Patriot leader who used hit-and-run attacks, known as guerilla warfare

Comte de Rochambeau commander of 4,000 French troops that aided the Patriot forces at the Battle of Yorktown

Battle of Yorktown the last major battle of the American Revolution

Treaty of Paris of 1783 the peace agreement in which Great Britain recognized the independence of the United States

Section Summary

WAR IN THE SOUTH

The war in the northern colonies did not go as the British government had hoped. The northern Patriots were tough to beat. The British moved the war into the South, where they believed large groups of Loyalists would help them win. General Henry Clinton led the British troops. The British plan worked at first.

> **Why did the British move the war to the South?**
> _____
> _____

The war in the South proved especially nasty. Patriots and Loyalists engaged in direct fighting. The British wiped out crops, farm animals, and property. Georgia fell to the British. Next, the British conquered the port of Charleston, South Carolina. The Patriots failed to retake Camden, South Carolina.

> **Underline the sentence that explains how the British army waged war in the South.**

Patriot General Nathanael Greene arrived to shape up the army. Meanwhile, under the leadership of **Francis Marion**, the Southern patriots used surprise attacks to cut off British communication and supply lines. The British could not capture Marion and his men.

> **How did Francis Marion and his men evade the British?**
> _____
> _____

Copyright © by Holt, Rinehart and Winston. All rights reserved.

Interactive Reader and Study Guide

BATTLE OF YORKTOWN

The Patriots were in trouble in early 1781. They had little money for paying soldiers and buying supplies. The British held most of the South as well as Philadelphia and New York.

The Continental Army began to pressure the British in the Carolinas. General Charles Cornwallis moved his 7,200 men to Yorktown, Virginia. In New York, General Washington combined his troops with French troops commanded by **Comte de Rochambeau**. Washington marched his force to Virginia in hopes of trapping Cornwallis in Yorktown.

With 16,000 soldiers, Washington's force surrounded Cornwallis. For weeks the French-American force wore down the British troops. Finally, the British surrendered. The Patriots captured 8,000 British prisoners at the **Battle of Yorktown**.

> What was Cornwallis's mistake in battle strategy?
> _____
> _____

THE TREATY OF PARIS

Britain lost most of its army at Yorktown and could not afford a new one. So Great Britain and America began peace talks. Delegates took more than two years to reach a peace agreement.

The Treaty of Paris of 1783 gave the United States independence from Great Britain. It also created America's borders. In a separate treaty, Britain returned Florida to the Spanish. The Patriots' courage had won the Revolutionary War.

> Why might reaching a peace treaty have taken so long?
> _____
> _____

CHALLENGE ACTIVITY

Critical Thinking: Predict Imagine that the Patriots had lost the Revolutionary War. Help lead a class discussion on how your lives would be different today.

Copyright © by Holt, Rinehart and Winston. All rights reserved.

Forming a Government

CHAPTER SUMMARY

Early U.S. Government

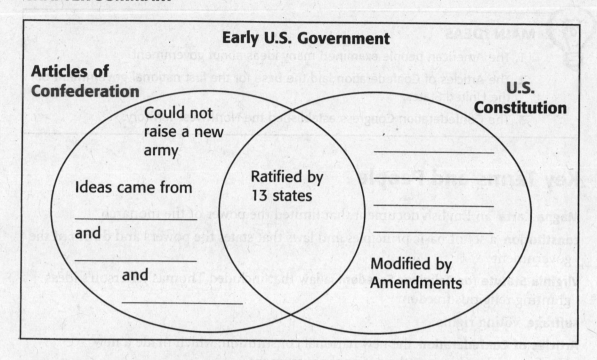

Articles of Confederation

- Could not raise a new army
- Ideas came from _____ and _____ and _____

Ratified by 13 states

U.S. Constitution

- _____
- _____
- _____

Modified by Amendments

COMPREHENSION AND CRITICAL THINKING

As you read the section summaries, fill in the blanks in the graphic organizer above and answer the questions below.

1. Identify What sources gave Americans ideas for their first national government under the Articles of Confederation?

_____

_____

_____

2. Compare and Contrast Describe four ways in which the U.S. Constitution was different from the Articles of Confederation.

_____

_____

_____

_____

Copyright © by Holt, Rinehart and Winston. All rights reserved.

Name _____ Class _____ Date _____

Forming a Government

MAIN IDEAS
1. The American people examined many ideas about government.
2. The Articles of Confederation laid the base for the first national government of the United States.
3. The Confederation Congress established the Northwest Territory.

Key Terms and People

Magna Carta an English document that limited the power of the monarch

constitution a set of basic principles and laws that states the powers and duties of the government

Virginia Statute for Religious Freedom a law that included Thomas Jefferson's ideas granting religious freedom

suffrage voting rights

Articles of Confederation the new national constitution, which made a new Confederation Congress the national government

ratification official approval of the Articles of Confederation by the states

Land Ordinance of 1785 a law that set up a system for surveying land and dividing the Northwest Territory

Northwest Ordinance of 1787 a law that established the Northwest Territory and formed a political system for the region

Northwest Territory a territory including Illinois, Indiana, Michigan, Ohio, and Wisconsin

Section Summary

IDEAS ABOUT GOVERNMENT

After winning independence from Great Britain, the United States needed to form new governments. The Americans first looked to English law for ideas. The English Bill of Rights and **Magna Carta** gave them inspiration. Ideas from the Enlightenment also influenced them. English philosopher John Locke had thought the government had a duty to guard people's rights.

> **Where did Americans find ideas for their government?**
> _____
> _____

Copyright © by Holt, Rinehart and Winston. All rights reserved.

Section 1, *continued*

In 1639 the people of Connecticut had created a government plan considered to be the first written **constitution** in the colonies. During the American Revolution nearly every state wrote a constitution to ensure that citizens elected representatives to make laws. **Suffrage** varied considerably from state to state. Some constitutions banned slavery. The **Virginia Statute for Religious Freedom** was an example of a law providing religious freedom.

> Should the states that banned slavery have been more insistent that other states ban it also? Why or why not?
> _____
> _____
> _____

ARTICLES OF CONFEDERATION

The Continental Congress named a Committee of Thirteen, with one member from each colony. This committee drafted the **Articles of Confederation**.

Under the Articles the Confederation Congress had limited powers to guard the people's freedoms. Each state had one vote in the Congress. The Congress had powers, but it could only ask the states for money and soldiers. States could refuse these requests. After some conflicts the Articles were **ratified** by all the states to form the first American government.

> Why would you have voted for or against the Articles?
> _____
> _____

NORTHWEST TERRITORY

Congress decided to raise money to pay debts by selling the ordinance lands. Congress passed the **Land Ordinance of 1785**. The **Northwest Ordinance of 1787** formed the **Northwest Territory**. It was then split up into several smaller territories. When the population of a territory hit 60,000, its settlers could draft their own constitution and ask to join the Union. Slavery was banned in the Northwest Territory.

> Underline the sentence that explains when a territory could ask to join the Union.

CHALLENGE ACTIVITY

Critical Thinking: Elaborating You plan to settle in the Northwest Territory. List 10 items you will take with you and explain why you chose the items you did.

Copyright © by Holt, Rinehart and Winston. All rights reserved.

43

Forming a Government

MAIN IDEAS
1. The United States had difficulties with other nations.
2. Internal economic problems plagued the new nation.
3. Shays's Rebellion pointed out weaknesses in the Articles of Confederation.
4. Many Americans called for changes in the national government.

Key Terms and People

tariffs taxes on imports or exports

interstate commerce trade between two or more states

inflation increased prices combined with the reduced value of money

depression a period of low economic activity combined with a rise in unemployment

Daniel Shays a poor farmer and Revolutionary War veteran

Shays's Rebellion an uprising in which Daniel Shays led hundreds of men in a forced shutdown of the Supreme Court in Springfield, Massachusetts

Section Summary

RELATIONS WITH OTHER COUNTRIES

The Continental Army broke up soon after the signing of the Treaty of Paris of 1783. The Articles of Confederation provided no way to raise a new army. The United States had a hard time guarding against foreign threats.

> Point out one weakness in the Articles of Confederation.
> _____
> _____

Problems arose in trading with Britain, which closed many British ports to U.S. ships. The British also forced American merchants to pay high **tariffs**. U.S. merchants increased prices to pay them, and costs were passed on to customers.

> Why did tariffs hurt U.S. citizens?
> _____
> _____

In 1784 Spanish officials shut down the lower Mississippi River to U.S. shipping. Western farmers and merchants used the river to ship goods east and overseas. The U.S. government failed to work out an agreement with Spain. Critics thought Spain would have negotiated longer if America had a strong military force. The loss of the British West Indies markets meant farmers could not sell goods there.

Copyright © by Holt, Rinehart and Winston. All rights reserved.

Interactive Reader and Study Guide

U.S. exports dropped while lower-priced British goods kept entering America. Congress could not pass tariffs.

ECONOMIC PROBLEMS

Trade problems among the states, war debt, and a poor economy hurt the states. The Confederation Congress had no power to regulate **interstate commerce**. States looked out only for their own trade interests.

> Underline the sentence that lists problems facing the states.

In addition, states had trouble paying off war debts. They printed paper money, but it had no gold or silver backing and little value. This caused **inflation**, which occurs when increased prices for goods and services combine with the reduced value of money. The loss of trade with Britain coupled with inflation created a **depression**.

> What conditions caused a depression in the United States?
>
> _____
>
> _____

SHAYS'S REBELLION

Massachusetts collected taxes on land to pay its war debt. This policy hurt farmers who owned land. The courts made them sell their property to pay taxes. **Daniel Shays** and his followers defied a state order that would stop **Shays's Rebellion**. They were defeated by state troops, and 14 leaders were sentenced to death. However, the state freed most, including Shays. Many citizens agreed with Shays.

CALLS FOR CHANGE

The weaknesses of the Confederation government led leaders, including James Madison and Alexander Hamilton, to ask all 13 states to send delegates to a Constitutional Convention. It was held in Philadelphia in May 1787 to revise the Articles of Confederation and create a better constitution.

CHALLENGE ACTIVITY

Critical Thinking: Predicting Consider how the new U.S. Constitution might change the Articles of Confederation. List three key changes.

Copyright © by Holt, Rinehart and Winston. All rights reserved.

Interactive Reader and Study Guide

Forming a Government

MAIN IDEAS
1. The Constitutional Convention met to improve the government of the United States.
2. The issue of representation led to the Great Compromise.
3. Regional debate over slavery led to the Three-Fifths Compromise.
4. The U.S. Constitution created federalism and a balance of power.

Key Terms and People

Constitutional Convention meeting held in Philadelphia to create a new constitution

James Madison a leading convention delegate from Virginia

Virginia Plan a plan giving supreme power to the central government and creating a bicameral legislature made of two groups, or houses, of representatives

New Jersey Plan a plan creating a unicameral, or one-house, legislature

Great Compromise an agreement that gave each state one vote in the upper house of the legislature and a number of representatives based on its population in the lower house

Three-Fifths Compromise only three-fifths of a state's slaves were counted when deciding representation in Congress

popular sovereignty the idea that political power belongs to the people

federalism the sharing of power between a central government and the states

legislative branch a Congress of two houses that proposes and passes laws

executive branch the president and the departments that help run the government

judicial branch a system of all the national courts

checks and balances a system that keeps any branch of government from becoming too powerful

Section Summary

CONSTITUTIONAL CONVENTION

The **Constitutional Convention** met in May 1787 in Philadelphia, where America had declared independence. Twelve states sent delegates. Most delegates were educated and had served in state legislatures or Congress. **James Madison** attended.

> Name one reason Philadelphia was chosen as the site of the Convention.
>
> _____
>
> _____

GREAT COMPROMISE

States disagreed about representation, tariffs, slavery, and strength of the central government. In the

Copyright © by Holt, Rinehart and Winston. All rights reserved.

Interactive Reader and Study Guide

Section 3, continued

Virginia Plan, the legislature would be selected on the basis of population. The New Jersey Plan proposed that each state receive an equal number of votes. The Great Compromise gave every state, regardless of size, an equal vote in the upper house of the legislature. Each state would be represented in the lower house based on population.

THREE-FIFTHS COMPROMISE

The Three-Fifths Compromise satisfied northerners, who wanted the number of slaves in southern states to determine taxes but not representation. It also satisfied southern delegates, who wanted slaves counted as part of their state populations to increase their power. The delegates agreed to end the slave trade in 20 years.

> Underline the sentence that explains what action about slavery the delegates took.

THE LIVING CONSTITUTION

The delegates wanted to protect popular sovereignty. They thought federalism could accomplish that. States would control government functions not assigned to the federal government.

The Constitution balances power among the legislative branch, the executive branch, and the judicial branch. The Constitution's framers established checks and balances to prevent any one branch from becoming too strong. The Constitution was completed in September 1787. Congress and then the states ratified the Constitution.

> What do you think about checks and balances?
> _____
> _____
> _____

CHALLENGE ACTIVITY

Critical Thinking: Making Judgments Decide whether you support the Three-Fifths Compromise. Give a two-minute speech about your view.

Copyright © by Holt, Rinehart and Winston. All rights reserved.

Interactive Reader and Study Guide

Forming a Government

> **MAIN IDEAS**
>
> 1. Federalists and Antifederalists engaged in debate over the new Constitution.
> 2. The *Federalist Papers* played an important role in the fight for ratification of the Constitution.
> 3. Ten amendments were added to the Constitution to provide a Bill of Rights to protect citizens.

Key Terms and People

Antifederalists people who opposed the Constitution

George Mason delegate who opposed the Constitution

Federalists people who supported the Constitution

Federalist Papers essays supporting the Constitution

amendments official changes to a document

Bill of Rights Constitutional amendments that protect the rights of citizens

Academic Vocabulary

advocate to plead in favor of

Section Summary

FEDERALISTS AND ANTIFEDERALISTS

Antifederalists believed that the Constitutional Convention should not have formed a new government. Delegate **George Mason** opposed the Constitution because it did not contain a section that guaranteed individual rights.

Most **Federalists** thought that the Constitution provided a good balance of power. Many wealthy planters, farmers, and lawyers were Federalists. Yet, many craftspeople, merchants, and poor workers also backed the Constitution. Several groups made speeches to **advocate** their views.

> Why did George Mason oppose the Constitution?
> _____
> _____
> _____

FEDERALIST PAPERS

The *Federalist Papers* were written anonymously by Alexander Hamilton, James Madison, and John Jay in defense of the Constitution. They tried to per-

Copyright © by Holt, Rinehart and Winston. All rights reserved.

Interactive Reader and Study Guide

suade people that the Constitution would not over-
whelm the states. Madison stated that the diversity
of the United States meant no single group would
take over the government.

The Constitution needed only nine states to pass
it, but each state should ratify it as a way of proclaim-
ing national unity. Every state except Rhode Island
held state conventions that gave citizens the right to
discuss and vote on the Constitution. On December
7, 1787, Delaware became the first state to ratify it.
The Constitution went into effect in June 1788 after
New Hampshire became the ninth state to ratify it.
Several states ratified the Constitution only after a
bill protecting individual rights was promised.

Why did states hold constitutional conventions?

_____

_____

What kind of bill did several states demand?

_____

BILL OF RIGHTS

Many Antifederalists did not believe that the
Constitution would safeguard personal rights.
In the first session of Congress, James Madison
spurred the legislators to develop a bill of rights.
The rights would then become **amendments** to
the Constitution after a two-thirds majority of
both houses of Congress and three-fourths of the
states approved them. Article V of the Constitution
spelled out this way of changing the document to
respond to the will of the people.

In December 1791 Congress proposed 12
amendments and turned them over to the states
for ratification. By December 1791 the states had
ratified the **Bill of Rights**. Ten of the proposed 12
amendments were written to protect citizens' rights.
These amendments show how the Constitution was
amended to meet the needs of a growing nation.

Why do you think the Constitution has lasted more than 200 years?

_____

_____

CHALLENGE ACTIVITY

Critical Thinking: Comparing and Contrasting Write a short essay comparing and contrasting the views of Federalists and Antifederalists. Use
specific examples.

Copyright © by Holt, Rinehart and Winston. All rights reserved.

Citizenship and the Constitution

CHAPTER SUMMARY

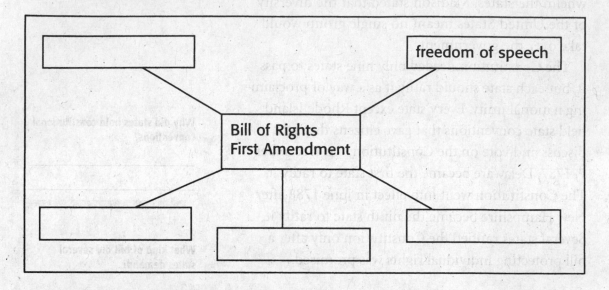

COMPREHENSION AND CRITICAL THINKING

As you read the section summaries, fill in the empty boxes above and answer the questions below.

1. Make Inferences How do you think James Madison felt about the possible dangers of majority rule?

_____

_____

_____

_____

2. Elaborate In what ways do you think that the First Amendment influences your life?

_____

_____

_____

_____

_____

_____

Copyright © by Holt, Rinehart and Winston. All rights reserved.

Citizenship and the Constitution

> **MAIN IDEAS**
> 1. The framers of the Constitution devised the federal system.
> 2. The legislative branch makes the nation's laws.
> 3. The executive branch enforces the nation's laws.
> 4. The judicial branch determines whether or not laws are constitutional.

Key Terms and People

federal system the government system that gives certain powers to the federal government

impeach vote to bring charges of serious crimes against a president

veto cancel

executive orders commands from the president that have the power of law

pardons orders from the president that grant freedom from punishment

Thurgood Marshall the first African American Supreme Court Justice, appointed in 1967

Sandra Day O'Connor the first female Supreme Court Justice, appointed in 1981

Academic Vocabulary

distinct separate

Section Summary

THE FEDERAL SYSTEM

Under the **federal system**, the U.S. Constitution divides powers between the states and the federal government. The Constitution gives the federal government delegated powers, including coining money. It gives state governments or citizens reserved powers, including forming local governments. Concurrent powers are shared by federal and state governments. These powers include taxing.

Congress has added powers under the elastic clause to handle new issues.

> **Describe concurrent powers.**
> _____
> _____

LEGISLATIVE BRANCH

The federal government has three branches, each with **distinct** responsibilities. Congress, the legislative

Copyright © by Holt, Rinehart and Winston. All rights reserved.

Interactive Reader and Study Guide

Section 1, *continued*

branch, has two parts. The House of Representatives has 435 members. A state's population determines the number of representatives for that state. Each state has two senators. They are elected statewide and represent the interests of the entire state.

What determines each state's number of representatives?
_____
_____

EXECUTIVE BRANCH

This branch enforces laws made by Congress. The president heads the branch. Americans elect a president every four years. Presidents are limited to two terms. The House of Representatives can **impeach** the president. The Senate tries the cases. Congress dismisses the president if he or she is found guilty.

The president and Congress work together. A president can **veto** a law passed by Congress. Congress can undo a veto with a two-thirds majority vote. The president issues **executive orders** to carry out laws affecting the Constitution and other areas. The president also issues **pardons**.

How can Congress undo a presidential veto?
_____
_____

JUDICIAL BRANCH

A system of federal courts with the U.S. Supreme Court at the head makes up this branch. Federal courts can undo a state or federal law if the court finds it unconstitutional. Congress can then change the law to make it constitutional.

If someone thinks a conviction was unfair, he or she can take the case to the court of appeals. The losing side in that trial may appeal the decision to the U.S. Supreme Court. If the Court declines to hear a case, the court of appeals decision is final. The Supreme Court has become more diverse with the appointments of **Thurgood Marshall** and **Sandra Day O'Connor**.

Why might a president appoint more diverse Justices?
_____
_____

CHALLENGE ACTIVITY

Critical Thinking: Judging Would you prefer to serve in the House or the Senate during an impeachment? Write a brief essay explaining why.

Copyright © by Holt, Rinehart and Winston. All rights reserved.

Citizenship and the Constitution

MAIN IDEAS

1. The First Amendment guarantees basic freedoms to individuals.
2. Other amendments focus on protecting citizens from certain abuses.
3. The rights of the accused are an important part of the Bill of Rights.
4. The rights of states and citizens are protected by the Bill of Rights.

Key Terms and People

James Madison a Federalist who promised that a Bill of Rights would be added to the Constitution

majority rule the idea that the greatest number of people in a society can make policies for everyone

petition a request made of the government

search warrant an order authorities must get before they search someone's property

due process a rule that the law must be fairly applied

indict formally accuse

double jeopardy a rule that says a person cannot be tried for the same crime more than once

eminent domain the government's power to take personal property to benefit the public

Section Summary

FIRST AMENDMENT

James Madison began writing a list of amendments to the Constitution in 1789. The states ratified 10 amendments, called the Bill of Rights. **Majority rule** could take away smaller groups' rights. The Bill of Rights protects all citizens. First Amendment rights include freedom of religion, freedom of the press, freedom of speech, freedom of assembly, and the right to **petition**. The U.S. government cannot support or interfere with the practice of a religion.

The freedoms of speech and the press give Americans the right to express their own ideas and hear those of others. Freedom of assembly means Americans may hold lawful meetings. Citizens can petition for new laws.

What does the Bill of Rights do?

_____

_____

Copyright © by Holt, Rinehart and Winston. All rights reserved.

PROTECTING CITIZENS

The Second, Third, and Fourth Amendments stem from colonial problems with Britain. The Second Amendment gives state militias the right to bear arms in emergencies. The Third Amendment protects citizens against housing soldiers. The Fourth Amendment protects against certain "searches and seizures." Authorities must obtain a **search warrant** to enter a citizen's property.

> When is a search warrant needed?
> _____
> _____

RIGHTS OF THE ACCUSED

The Fifth, Sixth, Seventh, and Eighth Amendments guard the rights of the accused. The Fifth Amendment says that the government cannot take a person's life, liberty, or property without **due process**. A grand jury decides whether to **indict** a person. No one can face **double jeopardy**. Under **eminent domain** the government must pay owners a fair amount for their property.

> Predict a situation in which a government might exercise its right of eminent domain.
> _____
> _____
> _____

The Sixth Amendment protects an indicted person's rights. The Seventh Amendment says that juries can decide civil cases, usually about money or property. The Eighth Amendment allows bail, or money defendants pay if they fail to appear in court. This amendment also prevents "cruel and unusual punishments" against a person convicted of a crime.

RIGHTS OF STATES AND CITIZENS

The Ninth Amendment states that all citizens' rights are not given by the Constitution. According to the Tenth Amendment, any powers not delegated to the federal government or prohibited to the states are held by the states and the people.

> What powers are held by the states and the people?
> _____
> _____

CHALLENGE ACTIVITY

Critical Thinking: Developing In a small group, draw up a new law for which you would like to petition a government official.

Copyright © by Holt, Rinehart and Winston. All rights reserved.

Citizenship and the Constitution

Section 3

MAIN IDEAS
1. Citizenship in the United States is determined in several ways.
2. Citizens are expected to fulfill a number of important duties.
3. Active citizen involvement in government and the community is encouraged.

Key Terms and People

naturalized citizens foreign-born people who: a) live in the United States, b) whose parents are not citizens, and c) who complete the requirements for U.S. citizenship

deport return to an immigrant's country of origin

draft required military service

political action committees groups that collect money for candidates who support certain issues

interest groups groups of people who share a common interest that motivates them to take political action

Academic Vocabulary

influence to change or have an effect on

Section Summary

GAINING U.S. CITIZENSHIP

Naturalized citizens of the United States may become full citizens. First, they apply for citizenship. Then they go through a process that leads to citizenship being granted. At that point, they have most of the rights and responsibilities of other citizens.

Legal immigrants have many of those rights and responsibilities but cannot vote or hold public office. The U.S. government can **deport** immigrants who break the law. Legal immigrants over age 18 may seek naturalization after living in the United States for five years. After completing the requirements, the person stands before a naturalization court and takes an oath of allegiance to the United States. They then receive certificates of naturalization. Two differences between native-born and naturalized citizens are that naturalized citizens can lose their

What limits exist on the rights of legal immigrants?
_____
_____

Where is the oath of allegiance taken?
_____
_____

Copyright © by Holt, Rinehart and Winston. All rights reserved.

Interactive Reader and Study Guide

Section 3, *continued*

citizenships, and they cannot become president or vice president.

DUTIES OF CITIZENSHIP

Citizens have duties as well as rights. Citizens must obey laws and authority. In addition, they must pay taxes for services, including public roads and public schools. Americans pay a tax on their income to the federal, and sometimes state, government. Men 18 years or older must register with selective service in case of a **draft**. Citizens must serve on juries to give others the right to a trial by jury.

> Why do citizens have duties along with rights?
> _____
> _____
> _____

CITIZENS AND GOVERNMENT

Voting in elections is one of a citizen's most important responsibilities. Before voting, a citizen must find out as much as possible about the issues and candidates. A variety of media sources offer information, but some may be deliberately biased.

> Underline the sentence that mentions media sources.

Anyone can help in a campaign, even people who are not eligible to vote. Many people help with donations to **political action committees** (PACs). People can **influence** government officials at any time. Many U.S. citizens work with **special interest groups**. Citizens can also work alone in elections or politics in general.

Many dedicated Americans also volunteer in community service groups, such as local firefighters or Neighborhood Watch groups that tell police if they see possible criminal activity in their area. Simple acts such as picking up trash in a park or serving food at a food shelter help a community.

> Why is community service important and valuable?
> _____
> _____
> _____

CHALLENGE ACTIVITY

Critical Thinking: Analyzing What connects a citizen's rights and responsibilities? Design a graphic organizer showing connections.

Copyright © by Holt, Rinehart and Winston. All rights reserved.

Interactive Reader and Study Guide

Launching the Nation

CHAPTER SUMMARY

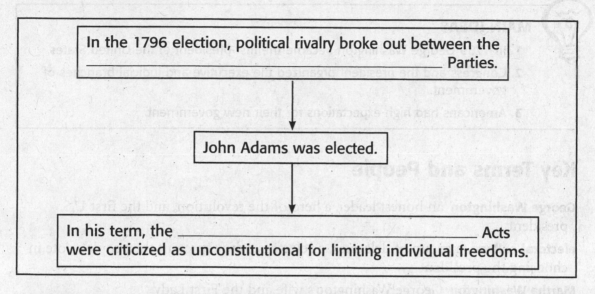

In the 1796 election, political rivalry broke out between the
_____ Parties.

John Adams was elected.

In his term, the _____ Acts
were criticized as unconstitutional for limiting individual freedoms.

COMPREHENSION AND CRITICAL THINKING

As you read the section summaries, fill in the blanks in the graphic
organizer above and answer the questions below.

1. Identify Which two parties were rivals in the 1796 presidential election?

_____

_____

_____

2. Describe Which two acts were criticized as unconstitutional during John Adams's
presidential term? Describe these acts.

_____

_____

_____

3. Make Judgments If you lived during Adams's term, what would you think about
the acts mentioned in Question 2?

_____

_____

_____

_____

Copyright © by Holt, Rinehart and Winston. All rights reserved.

Launching the Nation

MAIN IDEAS

1. In 1789 George Washington became the first president of the United States.
2. Congress and the president organized the executive and judicial branches of government.
3. Americans had high expectations for their new government.

Key Terms and People

George Washington an honest leader, a hero of the revolution, and the first U.S. president

electoral college a group of delegates, or electors, who represent the people's vote in choosing the president

Martha Washington George Washington's wife and the First Lady

precedent an action or a decision that later serves as an example

Judiciary Act of 1789 an act that created three levels of federal courts and defined their powers and relationships to the state courts

Academic Vocabulary

agreement a decision reached by two or more people or groups

Section Summary

THE FIRST PRESIDENT

George Washington was unanimously elected by the **electoral college** in January 1789. John Adams became his vice president. **Martha Washington** entertained and accompanied her husband at social events. She was in charge of the presidential household. Other women, such as Abigail Adams, wife of John Adams, believed women needed to play a larger role in the nation than Martha Washington did. They thought that women should take a more important role in society because they educated their children to be good citizens.

> Why did some women support a larger national role for women?
>
> _____
> _____
> _____

ORGANIZING THE GOVERNMENT

The new federal government had to establish a **precedent** when creating policies and procedures

Copyright © by Holt, Rinehart and Winston. All rights reserved.

Interactive Reader and Study Guide

Section 1, *continued*

that would have a great influence on the future of the nation. Congress formed departments in the executive branch to oversee various areas of national policy. Washington consulted with department heads, or cabinet members, who advised him. Our presidents today also meet with their key advisers.

Congress passed the **Judiciary Act of 1789**. This act created the federal court system and the courts' location. The president nominates candidates for federal judgeships. The Senate holds the power to approve or reject the candidates.

> **What did cabinet members provide for the president?**
> _____
> _____

> **What limited the president's ability to nominate federal judges?**
> _____
> _____
> _____

AMERICANS' EXPECTATIONS FOR THE NATION

Americans had high expectations of their government. They wanted trade that did not have the limits put in place by the British Parliament. They also expected the government to protect them and keep the economy strong.

In 1790 four million people lived in the United States. Most Americans worked on farms. They hoped for fair taxes and the right to move onto western lands. Americans who lived in towns worked as craftspeople, laborers, or merchants. They wanted help with their businesses. Merchants wanted simpler trade laws. Manufacturers wanted laws to shield them from overseas competitors.

> **Underline the sentences that explain the contrast between what country residents and town residents wanted.**

Most cities were small. Only New York and Philadelphia topped 25,000 residents. New York City, the first capital, reflected the new nation's spirit. In 1792 some 24 Wall Street stockbrokers signed an **agreement** that eventually created the New York Stock Exchange.

> **In what year was the agreement signed that led to the New York Stock Exchange?**

CHALLENGE ACTIVITY

Critical Thinking: Evaluating You have just attended George Washington's inauguration. Write a letter to a friend describing your thoughts about him.

Copyright © by Holt, Rinehart and Winston. All rights reserved.

Launching the Nation

MAIN IDEAS

1. Hamilton tackled the problem of settling national and state debt.

2. Thomas Jefferson opposed Hamilton's views on government and the economy.

3. Hamilton created a national bank to strengthen the U.S. economy.

Key Terms and People

Alexander Hamilton the first secretary of the U.S. treasury who wanted to pay the nation's foreign debt immediately and gradually repay the full value of all bonds

national debt money owed by the United States

bonds certificates that represent money

speculators people who buy items at low prices in the hope that the value will rise

Thomas Jefferson the first secretary of state who thought that repaying the full value of all bonds would cheat bondholders who had sold their bonds at low prices

loose construction the view that the federal government can take reasonable actions that the Constitution does not specifically forbid

strict construction the view that the federal government should do only what the Constitution specifically says it can do

Bank of the United States the national bank

Section Summary

SETTLING THE DEBT

Alexander Hamilton wanted to pay off the **national debt**. He figured that the United States owed $11.7 million to foreign countries. The nation also owed about $40.4 million to U.S. citizens.

During the Revolutionary War the government sold **bonds** to raise money. Officials said bonds would be repurchased at a higher price. Some bondholders sold their bonds to **speculators**. Hamilton and **Thomas Jefferson** disagreed on what to do. More politicians agreed with Hamilton. The government replaced old bonds with new, more reliable ones.

Hamilton thought that the federal government should repay $21.5 million of the states' debt. But southern leaders objected. Their states had rela-

> How did the government raise money during the Revolution?
>
> _____
>
> _____

Copyright © by Holt, Rinehart and Winston. All rights reserved.

Interactive Reader and Study Guide

tively low debts. Hamilton arranged to have the
U.S. capital's location changed from New York to
Philadelphia and finally Washington, D.C. Southern
leaders then supported his plan.

How did Hamilton persuade the southern leaders?
_____
_____

JEFFERSON OPPOSES HAMILTON

Hamilton and Jefferson disagreed about the role of
the central government. Hamilton wanted a strong
federal government. Jefferson wanted strong powers for the states. Hamilton did not want people
to have much power because he had little faith
in the average person. Jefferson believed that the
people had the right to rule the country. Hamilton
backed manufacturing, business, and higher tariffs.
Jefferson backed farming and lower tariffs.

Underline the sentences that explain Hamilton's and Jefferson's views of the American people.

A NATIONAL BANK

In 1791 Hamilton and Jefferson disagreed about the
government's economic problems. Hamilton wanted a national bank so the government could safely
deposit money. Jefferson believed that Hamilton's
plan gave too much power to the federal government. Hamilton supported **loose construction** of
the Constitution. Jefferson backed **strict construction**. Washington and Congress wanted the **Bank of
the United States**. It helped make the U.S. economy
more stable.

Name one reason Hamilton supported a national bank.
_____
_____

Do you think the Bank was a good idea? Why or why not?
_____
_____

CHALLENGE ACTIVITY

Critical Thinking: Evaluating Do you think Hamilton or Jefferson was
more correct in his views of people? Give a brief speech explaining your
opinion.

Copyright © by Holt, Rinehart and Winston. All rights reserved.

Launching the Nation

Section 3

MAIN IDEAS

1. The United States tried to remain neutral regarding events in Europe.
2. The United States and Native Americans came into conflict in the Northwest Territory.
3. The Whiskey Rebellion tested Washington's administration.
4. In his Farewell Address, President Washington advised the nation.

Key Terms and People

French Revolution a rebellion of the French people against their king that led to the creation of a republican government

Neutrality Proclamation a formal statement that the United States would not take sides with any European countries who were at war

privateers private ships hired by a country to attack its enemies

Jay's Treaty an agreement that settled the disputes between United States and Britain in the early 1790s

Pinckney's Treaty an agreement that settled border and trade disputes with Spain

Little Turtle a Native American chief who fought against U.S. forces in 1790

Battle of Fallen Timbers the battle that broke the strength of Native American forces in the Northwest Territory

Treaty of Greenville an agreement that gave the United States right of entry to American Indian lands

Whiskey Rebellion an uprising in which some farmers refused to pay the whiskey tax

Academic Vocabulary

neutral unbiased, not favoring either side in a conflict

Section Summary

REMAINING NEUTRAL

The **French Revolution** increased tensions between France and Britain. France and Great Britain finally went to war. George Washington believed the United States should be **neutral** and issued the **Neutrality Proclamation**. A French representative asked American sailors to command **privateers** to aid France in fighting England. Washington said that this violated U.S. neutrality. Jefferson thought the United States

> Why do you think some Americans supported the French Revolution?
>
> _____
>
> _____

Copyright © by Holt, Rinehart and Winston. All rights reserved.

Interactive Reader and Study Guide

Section 3, *continued*

should support France and resented interference in his role as secretary of state. He resigned in 1793.

Washington wanted to stop a war between the United States and Britain. The two sides signed **Jay's Treaty**. Britain would pay damages on seized American ships. Spain and the United States disputed the border of Florida. **Pinckney's Treaty** settled that issue and reopened New Orleans to American ships.

> **What did the United States gain from Pinckney's Treaty?**
> _____
> _____

CONFLICT IN THE NORTHWEST TERRITORY

Americans continued to settle the territory despite protests of American Indians. U.S. forces lost a battle to Miami chief **Little Turtle**. But General Anthony Wayne commanded U.S. troops in gaining the territory at last. The American Indians were defeated in the **Battle of Fallen Timber** and their leaders signed the **Treaty of Greenville** a year later.

> **Why might Americans Indians have protested the U.S. settlements?**
> _____
> _____

THE WHISKEY REBELLION

In March 1791 Congress passed a tax on American-made whiskey. The **Whiskey Rebellion** broke out. Washington personally led the army against the rebels in western Pennsylvania, but they fled. The revolt ended with no battle.

WASHINGTON SAYS FAREWELL

Washington declined to run for a third term. He had tired of public life and considered the American people the nation's leaders. In his farewell speech, he warned about the dangers of foreign ties and political conflicts at home. He also cautioned against too much debt. At the conclusion of his speech, he stated that he looked forward to a life "of good laws under a free government. . ."

> **Name two dangers that Washington mentioned.**
> _____
> _____

CHALLENGE ACTIVITY

Critical Thinking: Sequencing Create a timeline of important events in the 1790s. Describe each of the events and explain how one event caused or resulted from another event. Illustrate your timeline.

Copyright © by Holt, Rinehart and Winston. All rights reserved.

Interactive Reader and Study Guide

Launching the Nation

> **MAIN IDEAS**
> 1. The rise of political parties created competition in the election of 1796.
> 2. The XYZ affair caused problems for President John Adams.
> 3. Controversy broke out over the Alien and Sedition Acts.

Key Terms and People

political parties groups that help elect people and shape politics

Federalist Party a political group that wanted a strong federal government and supported industry and trade

Democratic-Republican Party a political group that wanted to limit the federal government's powers

XYZ affair a French demand for a $250,000 bribe and a $12 million loan in exchange for a treaty

Alien and Sedition Acts laws that punished supporters of France and deprived people of the freedom to say and write what they believed.

Kentucky and Virginia Resolutions formal statements that the Alien and Sedition Acts were unconstitutional

Section Summary

THE ELECTION OF 1796

In the election of 1796, more than one candidate ran for president. **Political parties** had started during Washington's presidency. Washington cautioned against party rivalry in his farewell, but rivalry dominated the 1796 election.

Alexander Hamilton was key in founding the **Federalist Party**. John Adams and Thomas Pinckney were the Federalist candidates. Thomas Jefferson and James Madison helped found the **Democratic-Republican Party**. That party selected Thomas Jefferson and Aaron Burr as its candidates.

Business people in cities tended to support Adams. Farmers generally favored Jefferson. Both sides attacked each other. Adams won; Jefferson was second. He and Jefferson then had to serve as president and vice president.

> Who helped start the Federalist Party?
>
> _____
>
> _____

Copyright © by Holt, Rinehart and Winston. All rights reserved.

PRESIDENT ADAMS AND THE XYZ AFFAIR

Adams made improving the relationship between the United States and France a high priority. France was unhappy when the United States refused to let its citizens join in the war against Britain. Adams sent U.S. diplomats to repair that problem and make a treaty to guard U.S. shipping. The French foreign minister refused to meet with them.

Three French agents said that the minister would discuss a treaty only if America paid a $250,000 bribe and gave a $12 million loan. The American public became furious about the **XYZ affair**. Still, Adams did not declare war on France. This angered many other Federalists. At last the United States and France did negotiate a peace treaty.

> Based on what you have read, what do you think Adams's view of France was?
>
> _____
>
> _____

> In the end, what occurred between the United States and France?
>
> _____
>
> _____

THE ALIEN AND SEDITION ACTS

The **Alien and Sedition Acts**, passed by Federalists in Congress, became law in 1798. The Alien Act empowered the president to remove foreign residents he decided were involved in any treasonable or secret plots against the government. The Sedition Act forbid U.S. residents to "write, print, utter, or publish" false or critical words against the government.

The **Kentucky and Virginia Resolutions** stated that the acts were unconstitutional. Jefferson and James Madison said that the states could disobey unconstitutional federal laws. Congress did not repeal the acts, though they were not renewed. The resolutions presented the view that states could dispute the federal government. Later politicians would say this idea meant that the states could declare laws or actions of the federal government to be illegal.

> Underline the sentence that explains what the Sedition Act did.

CHALLENGE ACTIVITY

Critical Thinking: Predicting Do some research to discover when in U.S. history states would say that they could declare federal law to be illegal. Write a brief essay explaining both sides of the argument.

Copyright © by Holt, Rinehart and Winston. All rights reserved.

Interactive Reader and Study Guide

The Jefferson Era

CHAPTER SUMMARY

Analyzing the War of 1812	
Reasons U.S. Entered War	1. British trade restrictions 2. 3.
Reasons U.S. Might Win	1. British at war with the French at the same time 2.
Reasons British Might Win	1. 2. White House burned

COMPREHENSION AND CRITICAL THINKING

As you read the section summaries, fill in the table above and answer the questions below.

1. Explain Why did the United States go to war with Britain in 1812?

_____

_____

_____

2. Evaluate If you were living at the time the war started, would you have felt confident that the United States would win the war? Why or why not?

_____

_____

_____

3. Draw a Conclusion How did the War of 1812 help the United States?

_____

_____

_____

_____

Copyright © by Holt, Rinehart and Winston. All rights reserved.

The Jefferson Era

MAIN IDEAS

1. The election of 1800 marked the first peaceful transition in power from one political party to another.

2. President Jefferson's beliefs about the federal government were reflected in his policies.

3. *Marbury* v. *Madison* increased the power of the judicial branch of government.

Key Terms and People

John Adams Federalist president first elected in 1796 who lost the 1800 presidential election

Thomas Jefferson Republican who defeated John Adams in the presidential election of 1800

John Marshall a Federalist appointed by Adams to be Chief Justice of the Supreme Court

Marbury* v. *Madison a case that established the Supreme Court's power of judicial review

judicial review the Supreme Court's power to declare an act of Congress unconstitutional

Academic Vocabulary

functions uses or purposes

Section Summary

THE ELECTION OF 1800

Thomas Jefferson defeated **John Adams** and became president in 1800. In campaigning, both sides had made their cases in newspaper editorials and letters. Both sides believed that if the other gained power, the nation would be destroyed.

The campaigning was intense. Federalists said if Jefferson gained power, revolution and chaos would follow. Republicans claimed that Adams would crown himself king. Jefferson and Aaron Burr, his vice presidential running mate, each won 73 votes. After the thirty-sixth ballot in the House of Representatives, Jefferson was elected President.

How did the presidential candidates wage the campaign of 1800?

_____

_____

Copyright © by Holt, Rinehart and Winston. All rights reserved.

JEFFERSON'S POLICIES

Jefferson gave his first speech in the new capitol.
He said he supported the will of the majority. He
emphasized his belief in a limited government and
the protection of civil liberties. Jefferson convinced
Congress to let the Alien and Sedition Acts expire.
He cut military spending to free money to pay the
national debt. The Republican-led Congress passed
laws to end the unpopular whiskey tax and other
domestic taxes.

> **Name one action Jefferson took based on his principles.**
> _____
> _____

In 1801 the national government was made up
of only several hundred people. Jefferson liked it
that way. He thought that safeguarding the nation
against foreign threats, delivering the mail, and
collecting custom duties were the most important
functions of the federal government. Jefferson had
fought Alexander Hamilton over the creation of the
Bank of the United States, but he did not close it.

MARBURY V. MADISON

Adams filled 16 new federal judgeships with
Federalists before leaving office. Republicans in
Congress soon repealed the Judiciary Act upon
which Adams's appointments were based. A controversy arose when Adams appointed William
Marbury as a justice of the peace. The documents
supporting Marbury's appointment were never
delivered.

When Jefferson took office, secretary of state
James Madison would not deliver them. Marbury
sued and asked the Supreme Court to order
Madison to give him the documents. **John Marshall**
wrote the Court's opinion in *Marbury* v. *Madison*.
He ruled that the law which Marbury's case depended upon was unconstitutional. The case established
the Court's power of **judicial review**.

> **Why did Marbury sue Madison?**
> _____
> _____

CHALLENGE ACTIVITY

Critical Thinking: Making Inferences What if the 1800 campaign were
waged as campaigns are waged now? Write a speech that you think Thomas
Jefferson would give. Deliver his speech.

Copyright © by Holt, Rinehart and Winston. All rights reserved.

Name _____ Class _____ Date _____

The Jefferson Era

MAIN IDEAS

1. As American settlers moved West, control of the Mississippi River became more important to the United States.

2. The Louisiana Purchase almost doubled the size of the United States.

3. Expeditions led by Lewis, Clark, and Pike increased Americans' understanding of the West.

Key Terms and People

Louisiana Purchase the purchase of Louisiana from France for $15 million, which roughly doubled the size of the United States

Meriwether Lewis a former army captain chosen by Jefferson to lead an expedition to explore the West

William Clark co-leader of the western expedition

Lewis and Clark expedition a long journey to explore the Louisiana Purchase

Sacagawea a Shoshone who helped the expedition by naming plants and gathering edible fruits and vegetables for the group

Zebulon Pike an explorer of the West who reached the summit of the mountain now known as Pike's Peak

Section Summary

AMERICAN SETTLERS MOVE WEST

Thousands of Americans moved into the area between the Appalachians and the Mississippi River. The setters used the Mississippi and Ohio rivers to move their products to eastern markets. Jefferson was concerned that a foreign power might shut down the port of New Orleans, which settlers needed to move their goods East and to Europe. Spain governed New Orleans and Louisiana, which extended from the Mississippi to the Rocky Mountains. Under a secret treaty, Spain gave Louisiana to France, transferring the problem of trying to keep Americans out of Louisiana.

> **Why did Jefferson worry about the port of New Orleans?**
> _____
> _____

> **Why would Americans want to move into Louisiana?**
> _____
> _____

Copyright © by Holt, Rinehart and Winston. All rights reserved.

Interactive Reader and Study Guide

LOUISIANA

In 1802, before giving Louisiana to France, Spain shut American shipping out of New Orleans. Jefferson sent U.S. representatives to France to buy New Orleans. Napoleon ruled France. He wanted to rebuild France's empire in North America. But Napoleon had no base for a conquest of Louisiana. He also needed money to wage war against Great Britain. The United States bought the western territory for $15 million in the **Louisiana Purchase**.

> What are two reasons that Napoleon did not try to conquer Louisiana?
> _____
> _____

EXPLORERS HEAD WEST

Western Native Americans and the land they lived on were a mystery. President Jefferson wanted to know about them and their land. He also wondered if there was a river route to the Pacific Ocean.

> Underline the sentences that explain why Jefferson wanted to know more about the West.

In 1803 Congress provided money to explore the West. **Meriwether Lewis** and **William Clark** were chosen to lead the **Lewis and Clark expedition**, which began in May 1804.

Lewis and Clark and their crew traveled up the Missouri River. Finally, they saw Native Americans, and Lewis used interpreters to tell their leaders that the United States now owned the land on which they lived. **Sacagawea** and her husband aided Lewis and Clark. Lewis and Clark did not find a river route to the Pacific, but they learned much about western lands.

In 1806 **Zebulon Pike** was sent to locate the Red River, which was the Louisiana Territory's border with New Spain. In present-day Colorado he reached the summit of Pike's Peak. Spanish cavalry arrested him in Spanish-held lands and imprisoned him. When released he returned to the United States and reported on his trip. He gave many Americans their first information about the Southwest.

> What are some of the difficulties faced by American expeditions in the West?
> _____
> _____

CHALLENGE ACTIVITY

Critical Thinking: Drawing Inferences Some members of the Lewis and Clark expedition kept journals or diaries. Write a brief diary entry as if you were a member of the expedition.

Copyright © by Holt, Rinehart and Winston. All rights reserved.

The Jefferson Era

MAIN IDEAS

1. Violations of U.S. neutrality led Congress to enact a ban on trade.
2. Native Americans, Great Britain, and the United States came into conflict in the West.
3. The War Hawks led a growing call for war with Great Britain.

Key Terms and People

USS Constitution a large U.S. warship sent to end attacks by Mediterranean pirates on American merchant ships

impressment the practice of forcing people to serve in the army or navy

embargo the banning of trade

Embargo Act a U.S. law that essentially banned trade with all foreign countries

Non-Intercourse Act a new law banning only trade with Great Britain, France, and their colonies

Tecumseh a brilliant speaker who warned other Native Americans that settlers wanted their lands

Battle of Tippecanoe the battle between the U.S. forces and Tecumseh's followers that ended with the U.S. forces winning

War Hawks several members of Congress who called for war against Great Britain

James Madison a Republican who was elected president in 1808

Section Summary

VIOLATIONS OF NEUTRALITY

In the late 1700s and early 1800s, American merchant ships sailed the oceans. The profitable overseas trade was dangerous. Pirates seized cargo and held crews for ransom. The United States sent the **USS Constitution** and other ships to end the attacks.

When Great Britain and France declared war in 1803, each tried to stop the United States from selling goods to the other. The British and French searched many American ships for war goods. Then Britain started searching American ships for sailors who had deserted the British navy. At times U.S. citizens were seized by accident.

> Why did Britain and France try to stop the United States from selling goods to the other?
>
> _____
>
> _____

Copyright © by Holt, Rinehart and Winston. All rights reserved.

Impressment continued over U.S. protests. Thomas Jefferson, who had been re-elected in 1804, favored an **embargo** rather than war with Britain. In late 1807 Congress passed the **Embargo Act** to punish Britain and France. American merchants lost huge amounts of money because of the act. In 1809 Congress replaced the embargo with the **Non-Intercourse Act**. That law did not work either.

> **How was an embargo an alternative to war?**
> _____
> _____

CONFLICT IN THE WEST

In the West, Native Americans, the United States, and Great Britain clashed. As settlers poured into the West, Native Americans lost land that they believed was taken unfairly. British agents from Canada armed Native Americans in the West. **Tecumseh**, a Shawnee chief, united his forces with the Creek nation. William Henry Harrison, the governor of the Indiana Territory, raised an army to battle Tecumseh. At the day-long **Battle of Tippecanoe**, Harrison's forces defeated the Native Americans.

> **How did British agents aid Native Americans in the West?**
> _____
> _____

CALL FOR WAR

War Hawks in Congress led in demanding war against Britain. The leaders wanted to end British influence on Native Americans. They resented British restraints on U.S. trade. Others opposed war against Britain. They believed America lacked the military strength to win.

In 1808 Republican **James Madison** was elected president. He had difficulty carrying on the unpopular trade policy. In 1812 he asked Congress to vote on whether to wage war against Britain. Congress voted to declare war. Madison was again elected. He became commander in chief in the War of 1812.

> **Describe the problem that Madison faced in 1808.**
> _____
> _____
> _____

CHALLENGE ACTIVITY

Critical Thinking: Predicting What difficulties might the United States face in the War of 1812? List them.

Copyright © by Holt, Rinehart and Winston. All rights reserved.

The Jefferson Era

MAIN IDEAS

1. American forces held their own against the British in the early battles of the war.
2. U.S. forces stopped British offensives in the East and South.
3. The effects of the war included prosperity and national pride.

Key Terms and People

Oliver Hazard Perry U.S. Navy commodore who won a victory against the British

Battle of Lake Erie the victory won by Perry and his sailors

Andrew Jackson the commander of the Tennessee militia who led an attack on the Creek nation in Alabama

Treaty of Fort Jackson the treaty that forced the Creek nation to give up millions of acres of their land

Battle of New Orleans the last major conflict of the War of 1812, which made Andrew Jackson a hero

Hartford Convention a meeting of Federalists opposed to the war

Treaty of Ghent the pact that ended the War of 1812

Academic Vocabulary

consequences the effects of a particular event or events

Section Summary

EARLY BATTLES

In 1812 the United States launched a war against a dominant nation. The British navy had hundreds of ships. The U.S. Navy had fewer than twenty ships, but it boasted expert sailors and big new warships. American morale rose when its ships defeated the British in several battles. Finally, the British blockaded U.S. seaports.

> Underline the sentences that contrast the U.S. and British navies.

The U.S. planned to attack Canada from Detroit, from Niagara Falls, and from the Hudson River Valley toward Montreal. British soldiers and Native Americans led by Tecumseh took Fort Detroit. State militia doomed the other two attacks against Canada by arguing that they were not required to fight in a foreign country.

Copyright © by Holt, Rinehart and Winston. All rights reserved.

In 1813 the United States planned to end Britain's rule of Lake Erie. Commodore **Oliver Hazard Perry** and his small fleet won the **Battle of Lake Erie**. General Harrison then marched his troops into Canada. He defeated a combined force of British and Native Americans, breaking Britain's power. Tecumseh died in the fighting, harming the alliance of the British and the Native Americans.

> **What effect did the death of Tecumseh have?**
> _____
> _____

In 1814 **Andrew Jackson** won a battle against the Creek nation that ended in the **Treaty of Fort Jackson**.

GREAT BRITAIN ON THE OFFENSIVE

The British sent more troops to America after defeating the French in 1814. The British set fire to the White House and other buildings in Washington, D.C. The British also attacked New Orleans.

Andrew Jackson commanded forces made up of regular soldiers. They included two battalions of free African Americans, a group of Choctaw Indian militia, and pirates led by Jean Lafitte. Although Jackson's forces were outnumbered, America won the **Battle of New Orleans**, the last key battle of the war. Andrew Jackson became a war hero.

> **Why was Andrew Jackson considered a hero?**
> _____
> _____

EFFECTS OF THE WAR

Before Federalist delegates from the **Hartford Convention** reached Washington, the war had ended. Slow communications meant that neither Jackson nor the Federalists heard that the **Treaty of Ghent** finished the war. Each nation gave back the territory it had conquered. Yet the war had **consequences**: intense patriotism in America as well as growth of American manufacturing.

> **In what ways did the war benefit the United States?**
> _____
> _____
> _____

CHALLENGE ACTIVITY

Critical Thinking: Drawing Inferences You are the first mate on a New England trading ship several months after the War of 1812. Write a letter about how the end of the war affects you.

Copyright © by Holt, Rinehart and Winston. All rights reserved.

Interactive Reader and Study Guide

A New National Identity

CHAPTER SUMMARY

COMPREHENSION AND CRITICAL THINKING

As you read the section summaries, complete the graphic organizer
above and answer the questions below.

1. Identify Cause and Effect How did the Monroe Doctrine contribute to America's
growing national identity?

_____

_____

_____

2. Identify Cause and Effect What was the goal of Henry Clay's American System?

_____

_____

_____

3. Draw Conclusions In what ways do you think the growing contributions of U.S.
culture increased the sense of national identity?

_____

_____

_____

Copyright © by Holt, Rinehart and Winston. All rights reserved.

A New National Identity

Section 1

MAIN IDEAS

1. The United States and Great Britain settled their disputes over boundaries and control of waterways.

2. The United States gained Florida in an agreement with Spain.

3. With the Monroe Doctrine, the United States strengthened its relationship with Latin America.

Key Terms and People

Rush-Bagot Agreement a compromise that limited U.S. and British naval power on the Great Lakes

Convention of 1818 a treaty that gave the United States fishing rights off parts of the Newfoundland and Labrador coasts

James Monroe U.S. president elected in 1816

Adams-Onís Treaty an agreement that settled all border disputes between the United States and Spain

Simon Bolívar the leader of the successful revolutions of Latin American colonies against Spain

Monroe Doctrine a statement of American policy warning European nations not to interfere with the Americas

Academic Vocabulary

circumstances surrounding situation

Section Summary

SETTLING DISPUTES WITH GREAT BRITAIN

After the War of 1812 ended, both the United States and Great Britain wanted to retain their navies and freedom to fish on the Great Lakes. The **Rush-Bagot Agreement** resolved that issue. The **Convention of 1818** gave America certain fishing rights, and it established the border between the United States and Canada. In this treaty, both countries agreed to occupy the Pacific Northwest together.

> What were the results of the Convention of 1818?
> _____
> _____

Copyright © by Holt, Rinehart and Winston. All rights reserved.

UNITED STATES GAINS FLORIDA

The United States also debated its border with Spanish Florida. President **James Monroe** sent General Andrew Jackson and troops to protect the U.S.-Florida border. Seminole Indians often aided runaway slaves and sometimes raided U.S. settlements. Under Jackson's command U.S. troops invaded Florida to catch Seminole raiders, starting the First Seminole War.

> Why did President Monroe send Jackson to Florida?
>
> _____
>
> _____

Jackson also captured most of Spain's key military posts. Jackson took these actions without a direct command from the president. The Spanish were upset, but most Americans backed Jackson. In 1819 Secretary of State John Quincy Adams and Spanish diplomat Luis de Onís negotiated the **Adams-Onís Treaty**. This treaty settled all border disputes between the United States and Spain.

> What convinced the Spanish to negotiate with the Americans?
>
> _____
>
> _____

MONROE DOCTRINE

By the early 1820s most Latin American countries had won independence from Spain. **Simon Bolívar**, called the Liberator, led many of these battles. The United States saw the **circumstances** as comparable to the American Revolution. United States leaders supported the Latin Americans in their struggles with European powers.

> Why did the United States support Latin American independence?
>
> _____
>
> _____

Monroe developed the **Monroe Doctrine** to guard against European countries interfering with the new Latin American nations. The document spells out the relationship between European nations and the United States in the Western Hemisphere. The doctrine states that the United States will intervene in Latin American affairs when American security is at risk. Few European nations challenged the doctrine.

CHALLENGE ACTIVITY

Critical Thinking: Cause and Effect Make a chart identifying the causes and effects of the Rush-Bagot Agreement, the Adams-Onís Treaty, and the Monroe Doctrine.

Copyright © by Holt, Rinehart and Winston. All rights reserved.

Interactive Reader and Study Guide

A New National Identity

Section 2

MAIN IDEAS

1. Growing nationalism led to improvements in the nation's transportation systems.
2. The Missouri Compromise settled an important regional conflict.
3. The outcome of the election of 1824 led to controversy.

Key Terms and People

nationalism a sense of pride and devotion to a nation

Henry Clay a U.S. representative from Kentucky who supported an emphasis on national unity

American System a series of measures intended to make the United States economically self-sufficient

Cumberland Road the first road built by the federal government

Erie Canal a waterway that ran from Albany to Buffalo, New York

Era of Good Feelings a U.S. era of peace, pride, and progress

sectionalism disagreement between leaders of different regions

Missouri Compromise an agreement that settled the conflict over Missouri's application for statehood

John Quincy Adams chosen as president by the House of Representatives in 1824

Academic Vocabulary

incentive something that leads people to action

Section Summary

GROWING NATIONALISM

Americans appreciated a rising sense of **nationalism** based on favorable negotiations with foreign nations. **Henry Clay** firmly supported this nationalism. Clay developed the **American System** to help create a stronger national economy and reduce regional disagreements. He pushed for a protective tariff and a national bank that would back a single currency to encourage interstate trade. The tariff funds could help improve roads and canals.

> How would a single currency encourage interstate trade?
>
> _____
>
> _____

Copyright © by Holt, Rinehart and Winston. All rights reserved.

The mainly dirt roads in the United States made travel hard in the early 1800s. The **Cumberland Road** stretched from Cumberland, Maryland, to Wheeling, on the Ohio River in present-day West Virginia. By 1850 its extension reached Illinois.

Construction of the **Erie Canal** started in 1817 and was finished in 1825. Water transportation was often faster, less expensive, and easier than road travel. Using shovels, British, German, and Irish immigrants dug the entire canal by hand. At that time the United States enjoyed an **Era of Good Feelings**. The canal's success was an **incentive** for a canal-building boom across the country.

> **Why were improvements in water transportation so important?**
> _____
> _____

MISSOURI COMPROMISE

Disagreements between the North and South, known as **sectionalism**, threatened the Union. When Missouri applied to enter the Union, the Union contained 11 free states and 11 slave states. The Senate's balance would favor the South if Missouri entered as a slave state.

Henry Clay persuaded Congress to agree to the **Missouri Compromise**. Missouri entered the Union as a slave state, and Maine entered as a free state. This kept an equal balance in the Senate. Slavery was banned in new territories or states north of Missouri's southern border.

> **How did Henry Clay help Missouri enter the Union?**
> _____
> _____

THE ELECTION OF 1824

Senator Andrew Jackson gained the most popular votes but not enough electoral votes to win the election. The House of Representatives chose **John Quincy Adams** as president. Jackson's supporters claimed that Adams had made a "corrupt bargain" with Representative Henry Clay to win. Later, Adams named Clay secretary of state. The election controversy cost Adams support among Americans.

> **How did Andrew Jackson lose the election of 1824?**
> _____
> _____

CHALLENGE ACTIVITY

Critical Thinking: Drawing Conclusions Would you support Adams despite the Clay controversy? Why or why not?

Copyright © by Holt, Rinehart and Winston. All rights reserved.

A New National Identity

Section 3

┌───┐
MAIN IDEAS

1. American writers created a new style of literature.

2. A new style of art showcased the beauty of America and its people.

3. American ideals influenced other aspects of culture, including religion and music.

4. Architecture and education were affected by cultural ideals.
└───┘

Key Terms and People

Washington Irving one of the first American writers to gain international fame

James Fenimore Cooper perhaps the best known of the new American writers

Hudson River school a group of artists whose paintings reflected national pride and an appreciation of the American landscape

Thomas Cole a landscape painter who was a founder of the Hudson River school

George Caleb Bingham an artist whose paintings showed both the American landscape and scenes from people's daily lives

Section Summary

AMERICAN WRITERS

Americans expressed their thoughts and feelings in literature and art. They took spiritual comfort in religion and music. The strengthening national identity was shown in education and architecture.

Washington Irving often wrote about American history. He cautioned Americans to learn from the past and prepare for the future. He often used a humorous style of writing called satire. In "Rip Van Winkle," one of his most famous short stories, Irving expresses his idea that Americans must use past lessons to deal with the future.

James Fenimore Cooper wrote about characters who lived on the frontier, including Native Americans. By placing some characters in historical events, he popularized historical fiction.

> **What was Irving's message?**
> _____
> _____

Copyright © by Holt, Rinehart and Winston. All rights reserved.

A NEW STYLE OF ART

The works of Irving and Cooper inspired painters. By the 1830s the **Hudson River school** had
appeared. **Thomas Cole** portrayed the American
landscape's unique traits. Other painters followed
his lead. **George Caleb Bingham** created a painting
that shows the rough lives of western traders as well
as the landscape.

> **Why did Bingham show the West as a rough place to live?**
> _____
> _____

RELIGION AND MUSIC

Religious revivalism fanned out across America
through the early and mid-1800s. Leaders met with
large crowds to reawaken religious faith. People
sang songs known as spirituals at revival meetings.
Spirituals are a kind of folk hymn from both white
and African American music traditions. Popular
folk music showed the unique views of the nation.
"Hunters of Kentucky" honored the Battle of New
Orleans. It was used successfully in the presidential
campaign of Andrew Jackson in 1828.

> **How were spirituals important for religious revival meetings?**
> _____
> _____

ARCHITECTURE AND EDUCATION

In pre-Revolution America, most American architects modeled their designs on the style used
in Great Britain. After the Revolution, Thomas
Jefferson said that Americans should base their
building designs on those of ancient Greece and
Rome. Many architects agreed with Jefferson and
used Greek and Roman styles.

Americans also found education important. In
1837 Massachusetts set up a state board of education. Other states followed Massachusetts and started their own education systems.

> **Why did Jefferson want Americans to change their styles of architecture?**
> _____
> _____

CHALLENGE ACTIVITY

Critical Thinking: Elaborating Would you prefer to be a writer or a
landscape artist? Make a choice, and either write an essay describing the
western American landscape in the 1800s or draw a picture of it.

Copyright © by Holt, Rinehart and Winston. All rights reserved.

The Age of Jackson

CHAPTER SUMMARY

CAUSE		EFFECT
More people received the right to vote.	⟶	
	⟶	Northerners supported tariffs.
	⟶	Southerners opposed tariffs.
The United States wanted to control more land.	⟶	The Indian Removal Act passed in 1830.

COMPREHENSION AND CRITICAL THINKING

As you read the section summaries, fill in the table above and answer the questions below.

1. Explain Give one reason that the political system changed in the early 1800s.

_____

_____

_____

_____

_____

_____

2. Identify Cause and Effect Why did most northerners support tariffs and most southerners oppose them?

_____

_____

_____

_____

_____

_____

_____

_____

Copyright © by Holt, Rinehart and Winston. All rights reserved.

Interactive Reader and Study Guide

The Age of Jackson

MAIN IDEAS
1. Democracy expanded in the 1820s as more Americans held the right to vote.
2. Jackson's victory in the election of 1828 marked a change in American politics.

Key Terms and People

nominating conventions public meetings to select a party's presidential and vice presidential candidates

Jacksonian Democracy the democratic expansion that occurred during Jackson's presidency

Democratic Party a party formed by Jackson supporters

John C. Calhoun Jackson's vice presidential running mate

spoils system the practice of rewarding political supporters with government jobs

Martin Van Buren the secretary of the state in Jackson's cabinet

Kitchen Cabinet an informal group of Jackson's trusted advisers that sometimes met in the White House kitchen

Section Summary

EXPANSION OF DEMOCRACY

In the early 1800s state legislatures expanded democracy, giving more people voting rights. However, women and African Americans still had no voting rights in most states.

By 1828 almost all states had changed the system under which state legislatures nominated electors in the electoral college. Now, the people nominated their own electors. Some parties began to hold **nominating conventions**. Broader voting rights and conventions allowed more people to actively participate in politics.

Andrew Jackson entered the political scene as American democracy grew. Historians called the expansion of democracy in this era **Jacksonian Democracy**.

> Who was left out in the push to give Americans more voting rights?
> _____
> _____

Copyright © by Holt, Rinehart and Winston. All rights reserved.

Interactive Reader and Study Guide

ELECTION OF 1828

Jackson's supporters were mainly farmers, frontier settlers, and southern slaveholders. They believed he would protect the rights of the common people and the slave states. They referred to themselves as Democrats and established the **Democratic Party**. Many supporters of President John Quincy Adams called themselves National Republicans.

> **Who supported Adams for president?**
> _____
> _____

The presidential candidates were President Adams and Andrew Jackson in a replay of the 1824 election. Jackson selected South Carolina Senator **John C. Calhoun** as his running mate. The campaign concentrated on personalities. Jackson's campaigners said he was a war hero who was born poor and earned success through hard work. They said that Adams knew nothing about everyday people because his father had been the second U.S. president. Adams's backers said Jackson was too coarse to be president.

> **What were some of the key differences between Jackson and Adams?**
> _____
> _____

Jackson and Calhoun won the election. Jackson's supporters described his victory as a triumph for the common people. A crowd of some 20,000 people held a big party on the White House lawn to celebrate. Jackson began the **spoils system**, but he replaced fewer than one-fifth of federal officeholders. One of Jackson's strongest cabinet members was **Martin Van Buren**. Jackson also relied heavily on a trusted group of advisors that was called the **kitchen cabinet**.

> **Why might so many people have attended the election party?**
> _____
> _____
> _____

CHALLENGE ACTIVITY

Critical Thinking: Analyze Make a chart contrasting facts about Adams and Jackson with people's opinions of them.

Copyright © by Holt, Rinehart and Winston. All rights reserved.

The Age of Jackson

Section 2

MAIN IDEAS

1. Regional differences grew during Jackson's presidency.
2. The rights of the states were debated amid arguments about a national tariff.
3. Jackson's attack on the Bank sparked controversy.
4. Jackson's policies led to the Panic of 1837.

Key Terms and People

Tariff of Abominations a tariff with very high rates

states' rights doctrine the belief that state power should be greater than federal power

nullification crisis the dispute over whether states had the right to nullify, or disobey, any federal law with which they disagreed

Daniel Webster a senator from Massachusetts who spoke out against nullification and believed the nation had to stay united

McCulloch v. Maryland the case in which the U.S. Supreme Court ruled that the Second Bank of the United States was constitutional

Whig Party a political group supported by people who opposed Andrew Jackson

Panic of 1837 a financial crisis that led to a severe economic depression

William Henry Harrison a general and the Whig presidential candidate in 1840

Academic Vocabulary

criteria basic requirements

Section Summary

SECTIONAL DIFFERENCES INCREASE

In Andrew Jackson's presidency, people's reaction to almost every policy was based on where they lived and the economy of their region. The North's economy depended on trade and manufacturing. The North supported tariffs, which helped it compete with foreign manufacturers. Southerners marketed a large portion of their crops to foreign countries. Most southerners opposed tariffs, which led to higher prices in manufactured items that they bought. Westerners wanted cheap land.

> **Why did northerners disagree with southerners on the issue of tariffs?**
>
> _____
>
> _____

Copyright © by Holt, Rinehart and Winston. All rights reserved.

Northerners continued to demand high tariffs to guard their new industries from foreign competition. In 1828 Congress passed a law that southerners called the **Tariff of Abominations**. (An abomination is a hateful thing.) The tariff intensified sectional differences.

> **How did the Tariff of Abominations help industries in the North?**
> _____
> _____

STATES' RIGHTS DEBATE

Vice President John C. Calhoun supported the **criteria** of a strong central government. Later on, he argued for the **states' rights doctrine**. The debate over states' rights led to the **nullification crisis**. Jackson opposed nullification. Calhoun resigned from office. South Carolina's legislature declared that a new 1832 tariff would not be collected in the state. **Daniel Webster** backed a unified nation. Congress finally agreed to lower the tariffs gradually. South Carolina's leaders agreed to obey the law but still backed the nullification idea.

> **What caused the nullification crisis?**
> _____
> _____

JACKSON ATTACKS THE BANK

President Jackson and many southern states questioned the constitutional legality of the Second Bank of the United States. However, in the case *McCulloch* v. *Maryland*, the Bank was found to be constitutional. Jackson moved most of the Bank's funds to state banks. This action caused inflation.

> **What happened when the federal bank's funds were moved to state banks?**
> _____
> _____

PANIC OF 1837

The **Whig Party** backed four candidates for president in 1836, and the Democrat, Martin Van Buren, won. When the country experienced the **Panic of 1837**, Van Buren was blamed. In 1840 the Whigs nominated **William Henry Harrison**, who won with an electoral landslide.

> **Why might voters have chosen Harrison over Van Buren?**
> _____
> _____

CHALLENGE ACTIVITY

Critical Thinking: Summarizing Design a poster that illustrates President Jackson's actions in his two terms. Use captions.

Copyright © by Holt, Rinehart and Winston. All rights reserved.

The Age of Jackson

MAIN IDEAS

1. The Indian Removal Act authorized the relocation of Native Americans to the West.

2. Cherokee resistance to removal led to disagreement between Jackson and the Supreme Court.

3. Other Native Americans resisted removal with force.

Key Terms and People

Indian Removal Act the act that authorized the removal of Native Americans who lived east of the Mississippi River

Indian Territory the new homeland for Native Americans, which contained most of present-day Oklahoma

Bureau of Indian Affairs an agency created to oversee the federal policy toward Native Americans

Sequoya a Cherokee who used 86 characters to represent Cherokee syllables to create a written language

Worcester* v. *Georgia a case in which the U.S. Supreme Court ruled that the state of Georgia had no authority over the Cherokee

Trail of Tears an 800-mile forced march westward in which one-fourth of the 18,000 Cherokee died

Black Hawk a Sauk chief who decided to fight rather than be removed

Osceola Seminole leader who called on Native Americans to resist removal by force

Academic Vocabulary

contemporary existing at the same time

Section Summary

INDIAN REMOVAL ACT

President Andrew Jackson's policies toward Native Americans were controversial. They had long lived in settlements from Georgia to Mississippi. Jackson and other political leaders wanted this land for American farmers. Jackson pressured Congress to pass the **Indian Removal Act** in 1830. The **Indian Territory** was set aside as a new home for Native Americans.

> Why were Jackson's policies toward Native Americans controversial?
> _____
> _____

Copyright © by Holt, Rinehart and Winston. All rights reserved.

Interactive Reader and Study Guide

Section 3, continued

The **Bureau of Indian Affairs** was estab-
lished. Indian peoples began to be removed to
Indian Territory. They lost their lands east of the
Mississippi. On their trips to Indian Territory, many
Native Americans died of cold, disease, and
starvation.

> Why was the Indian Territory established?
> _____
> _____

CHEROKEE RESISTANCE

The Cherokee adopted the **contemporary** culture of
white people to avoid conflicts. **Sequoya** helped the
Cherokee create their own written language.

The Cherokee sued the state when the Georgia
militia tried to remove them. In the case *Worcester
v. Georgia,* the U.S. Supreme Court ruled in favor
of the Cherokee. Georgia ignored the ruling and
removed the Cherokee. On the **Trail of Tears**, the
Cherokee suffered from heat, cold, and exposure.

OTHER NATIVE AMERICANS RESIST

Conflicts broke out in Illinois and Florida when
some Native Americans decided to resist removal.
Chief **Black Hawk** led the Sauk of Illinois in raiding settlements and fighting the U.S. Army. The U.S.
Army attacked the Sauk as they retreated, and the
uprising ended.

> How did the Sauk resist removal?
> _____
> _____

In Florida the Seminole also resisted removal. In
1832 some Seminole leaders were forced to sign a
treaty that said they would withdraw from Florida
in seven years. Any Seminole of African ancestry
would be called a runaway slave. The Seminoles
ignored the treaty. **Osceola** led his followers in the
Second Seminole War. The Seminole won many
battles. Some 1,500 U.S. soldiers died. After spending millions, U.S. officials gave up.

> How did the outcome for the Seminole differ from that of other Native Americans?
> _____
> _____

CHALLENGE ACTIVITY

Critical Thinking: Analyzing Write an essay explaining how your view
of the Indian Removal Act would compare or contrast with the view of
an easterner who wanted to settle on Native American lands.

Copyright © by Holt, Rinehart and Winston. All rights reserved.

Interactive Reader and Study Guide

Expanding West

CHAPTER SUMMARY

Date	Event
1811	John Jacob Astor founds Astoria
1819	Adams-Onís Treaty
1821	Agustin de Iturbide wins Mexican freedom
1830	Joseph Smith founds Church of Jesus Christ of the Latter-day Saints
1835	Texas Revolution begins in Gonzales
1836	
1839	John Sutter starts his colony in California
1844	Brigham Young leads Mormons to Utah
1846	Treaty with British gives U.S. all Oregon land south of 49th parallel
1846	
1847	Brigham Young founds Salt Lake City
1848	
1853	
1869	Transcontinental railroad completed

COMPREHENSION AND CRITICAL THINKING

As you read the section summaries, complete the table above and answer the questions below.

1. Recall and Identify Add the following events to the graphic organizer. Gadsden Purchase; California becomes 31st state; Fall of the Alamo; Bear Flag Revolt.

2. Sequence How many years passed between the first gathering of the Mormons and their final settlement in Utah?

_____

_____

_____

3. Evaluate Some would say that the events listed above demonstrate the validity of manifest destiny. Do you agree? Why or why not?

_____

_____

_____

_____

_____

Copyright © by Holt, Rinehart and Winston. All rights reserved.

Expanding West

MAIN IDEAS

1. During the early 1800s, Americans moved west of the Rocky Mountains to settle and trade.

2. The Mormons traveled west in search of religious freedom.

Key Terms and People

mountain men fur traders and trappers who traveled to the Rocky Mountains and the Pacific Northwest in the early 1800s

John Jacob Astor owner of the American Fur Company who founded the first important settlement in Oregon Country in 1811

Oregon Trail the main route from the Mississippi River to the West Coast in the early 1800s

Santa Fe Trail the route from Independence, Missouri, to Santa Fe, New Mexico

Mormons members of a religious group, formally known as the Church of Jesus Christ of Latter-day Saints, that moved west during the 1830s and 1840s

Brigham Young Mormon leader who chose Utah as the group's new home

Section Summary

AMERICANS MOVE WEST

In the early 1800s trappers and traders known as **mountain men** worked to supply the eastern fashion for fur hats and clothing. **John Jacob Astor**, owner of the American Fur Company, sent mountain men to the Pacific Northwest region that became known as Oregon Country. At this time Oregon Country was inhabited by Native Americans. However, it was claimed by Russia, Spain, Great Britain, and the United States.

In 1811 Astor founded Astoria, which was the first major non-Native American settlement in the region, at the mouth of the Columbia River. After a series of treaties, Oregon Country soon became jointly occupied by Great Britain and the United

> **What did mountain men do?**
> _____
> _____

> **Where was the first major non-native American settlement located?**
> _____
> _____

Copyright © by Holt, Rinehart and Winston. All rights reserved.

States. Many Americans began to move to the region, most of them following a challenging and dangerous route that became known as the **Oregon Trail**. It was common for families to band together and undertake the perilous six-month journey in wagon trains.

Another well-traveled route west, the **Santa Fe Trail**, was used mainly by traders. They loaded wagon trains with cloth and other manufactured goods that could be traded for horses, mules, and silver in the Mexican settlement of Santa Fe.

> What do you think was the main language spoken in Santa Fe at this time?
> _____

MORMONS TRAVEL WEST

One large group of settlers traveled west in search of religious freedom. Joseph Smith founded the Church of Jesus Christ of Latter-day Saints in 1830 in western New York state. Although church membership grew rapidly, the converts, known as **Mormons**, were dogged by local hostility. To protect his growing community from persecution, Smith led his followers to a series of settlements in Ohio, Missouri, and Illinois.

> Do some research on the Mormons. Trace the path that they took from New York to Salt Lake City.

When Smith was murdered by an anti-Mormon mob in 1844, **Brigham Young** led the Mormons to a desert valley near the Great Salt Lake in what is now Utah. There the Mormons planned and built Salt Lake City and settled in the area. By December 1860 the Mormon population of Utah stood at about 40,000.

> Using the library or an online resource, find out how many members worldwide the Mormon Church has today.
> _____

CHALLENGE ACTIVITY

Critical Thinking: Drawing Inferences Make a list of supplies that a family of four would need to make a six-month journey by wagon train through the American West during the 1830s.

Copyright © by Holt, Rinehart and Winston. All rights reserved.

Interactive Reader and Study Guide

Name _____ Class _____ Date _____

Expanding West

 MAIN IDEAS
1. Many American settlers moved to Texas after Mexico achieved independence from Spain.
2. Texans revolted against Mexican rule and established an independent nation.

Key Terms and People

Father Miguel Hidalgo y Costilla priest who led the first major Mexican revolt against Spanish rule in 1810

empresarios agents of the Mexican republic hired to bring settlers to Texas

Stephen F. Austin empresario who established the first American colony in Texas

Antonio López de Santa Anna Mexican leader who came to power in 1830 and suspended Mexico's constitution

Alamo an old mission in San Antonio occupied by Texan revolutionary forces in 1836

Battle of San Jacinto decisive victory that gave Texas independence from Mexico

Academic Vocabulary

explicit fully revealed without vagueness

Section Summary

AMERICAN SETTLERS MOVE TO TEXAS

In the early 1800s, the region we now know as the American Southwest was part of Mexico, which in turn was part of the vast Spanish empire in the Americas. Mexico struggled against Spanish rule. A revolt led by **Father Miguel Hidalgo y Costilla** in 1810 failed, but the rebellion he started grew. In 1821 Mexico became independent.

> During the early 1800s, in what part of Mexico was Texas located?
> _____
> _____

In order to establish control of Texas, the new Mexican republic hired agents known as **empresarios** to bring settlers there. One of these, **Stephen F. Austin**, selected a site on the lower Colorado River and settled 300 families, mostly from the southern states. These settlers often **explicitly** ignored Mexican laws, including Mexico's law forbidding slavery.

> Use an online browser or another resource to research "the Old 300."

Tension grew between Mexico's central government and the American settlers. Colonists were

> From what region of the United States did most settlers come to Texas?
> _____
> _____

Copyright © by Holt, Rinehart and Winston. All rights reserved.

Interactive Reader and Study Guide

angry when **Antonio López de Santa Anna** came to
power in 1830 and suspended Mexico's constitution.
Austin was imprisoned for a year and a half. When
he returned to Texas, he began urging Texans to
rebel against Mexico.

> Underline the sentence that helps explain why tension grew between the central Mexican government and the American settlers in Texas.

TEXANS REVOLT AGAINST MEXICO

Hostilities began with a battle at Gonzalez in 1835.
Santa Anna inflicted two brutal defeats on the
Texans at the **Alamo** and Goliad. Within a month,
however, Texas forces under Sam Houston had won
a decisive victory over Santa Anna at the **Battle of
San Jacinto**. Santa Anna signed a treaty giving Texas
its independence.

> Use the library or an online resource to find an account of the famous siege of the Alamo.

Most people in the new Republic of Texas hoped
that Texas would join the United States. However,
U.S. President Andrew Jackson was concerned about
two factors. He was worried that admitting Texas as
a slave state would upset the fragile balance between
free and slave states in the Union. Also, Jackson
feared that annexing Texas might lead to a war with
Mexico.

As the annexation of Texas was delayed, more
American settlers came from nearby southern states,
often bringing slaves with them to work the land
and to grow cotton. Tensions between Mexico and
Texas remained high. After a few unsettled years,
Texas President Sam Houston signed a peace treaty
with Mexico in 1844.

> What did many American settlers bring with them to Texas?
>
> _____
>
> _____

CHALLENGE ACTIVITY

Critical Thinking: Evaluation Take sides in a debate as to whether Texas
should join the United States or remain an independent nation. Write an
explicit defense of your position.

Copyright © by Holt, Rinehart and Winston. All rights reserved.

Expanding West

MAIN IDEAS

1. Many Americans believed that the nation had a manifest destiny to claim new lands in the West.

2. As a result of the Mexican-American War, the United States added territory in the Southwest.

3. American settlement in the Mexican Cession produced conflict and a blending of cultures.

Key Terms and People

manifest destiny belief that America's fate was to conquer land all the way to the Pacific Ocean

James K. Polk U.S. president, elected in 1844, whose administration annexed both Texas and Oregon

vaqueros cowboys

Californios Spanish colonists and their descendants living in California

Bear Flag Revolt rebellion of American settlers against the Californios in 1846

Treaty of Guadalupe Hidalgo 1848 peace treaty between Mexico and the United States

Gadsden Purchase purchase from Mexico of the southern parts of present-day New Mexico and Arizona in 1853

Academic Vocabulary

elements a basic part of an individual's surroundings

Section Summary

MANIFEST DESTINY

The idea of **manifest destiny** loomed large in the election of 1844. The new president, **James K. Polk**, promised to annex both Texas and Oregon.

In 1846 Britain and the United States signed a treaty that gave the United States all Oregon land south of the 49th parallel. This treaty drew the present-day border between the United States and Canada. In 1845 the congresses of both the Republic of Texas and the United States approved annexation of Texas.

After winning independence from Spain in 1821, Mexico began changing old policies set by Spain.

> Use the library or an online resource for an understanding of why the idea of manifest destiny may have been so attractive during the 1840s.

Copyright © by Holt, Rinehart and Winston. All rights reserved.

Interactive Reader and Study Guide

Mission lands were broken up into vast ranches. *Vaqueros* managed the herds of cattle and sheep. Settlers, known as **Californios**, felt little connection to their faraway government in Mexico. American settlers also began coming to California and calling for independence from Mexico.

> Did the Californios resent the arrival of large numbers of American settlers? Why or why not?
>
> _____
> _____
> _____

MEXICAN-AMERICAN WAR

Since the Texas Revolution the border between Mexico and Texas had been in dispute. Mexico claimed the border lay along the Nueces River while the United States claimed the Rio Grande as the border. In 1845 President Polk sent troops to the Rio Grande. When Mexican soldiers attacked them, Congress declared war on Mexico. Although many Americans thought the war was unjustified, U.S. troops pushed into Mexico, going from victory to victory until they finally captured Mexico City. A successful revolt against the Californios in Sonoma, known as the **Bear Flag Revolt**, proclaimed California to be an independent nation.

> Some Americans at the time thought President Polk provoked the Mexican attack by stationing soldiers on the Rio Grande. Do you agree? Explain your answer.
>
> _____
> _____

> Use the library or an online resource to find a map showing the territorial growth of the United States during this period.

AMERICAN SETTLEMENT IN THE MEXICAN CESSION

The **Treaty of Guadalupe Hidalgo**, which ended the Mexican War in 1848, increased the land area of the United States by almost 25 percent. A few years later, in 1853, the **Gadsden Purchase** fixed the continental boundaries of the United States.

As American settlers flooded the Southwest, the **elements** of life changed. Cultural encounters often led to conflict and violence. New settlers usually ignored Mexican legal ideas, such as community property and water rights. However, traditional knowledge and customs gradually shaped local economies, and new and mutually beneficial trade patterns began to emerge.

> Why is the issue of water rights much more serious in the West than it is in the East?
>
> _____
> _____
> _____

CHALLENGE ACTIVITY

Critical Thinking: Identify Cause and Effect Write a law regulating water rights.

Copyright © by Holt, Rinehart and Winston. All rights reserved.

Interactive Reader and Study Guide

Expanding West

MAIN IDEAS
1. The discovery of gold brought settlers to California.
2. The gold rush had a lasting impact on California's population and economy.

Key Terms and People

John Sutter Swiss immigrant who started the first Anglo-Californian colony in 1839

Donner party a group of western travelers who were trapped crossing the Sierra Nevada Mountains in the winter of 1846–47

forty-niners gold-seeking migrants who traveled to California in 1849

prospect search for gold

placer miners miners who used pans or other devices to wash gold nuggets from loose rock or gravel

Section Summary

DISCOVERY OF GOLD BRINGS SETTLERS

Before 1840 few Americans settled in California, although there was considerable trade between merchants from Mexico and the United States. However, after Mexico allowed **John Sutter** to establish a colony in 1839, American settlers began arriving in greater numbers. In a tragic incident, heavy snows in the Sierra Nevada Mountains trapped a group of travelers known as the **Donner party**. Half of the travelers either froze or starved to death.

When gold was discovered at Sutter's Mill in 1848, the news spread across the country. During 1849 about 80,000 **forty-niners** came to California hoping to strike it rich. Most of them arrived in the small port town of San Francisco. Within a year, the population of San Francisco grew from around 800 to more than 25,000.

Mining methods varied by the time of year and the location of the claim. **Placer miners** would **prospect** by using pans or other devices to wash gold nuggets out of the loose rock and gravel. Richer miners established companies to dig shafts and tunnels. Many individual success stories

> **What country was California part of in 1840?**
> _____
> _____

> **Would mining experience have helped the average forty-niner? Explain your answer.**
> _____
> _____
> _____
> _____

Copyright © by Holt, Rinehart and Winston. All rights reserved.

Interactive Reader and Study Guide

inspired prospectors. However, the good luck that made some miners wealthy never came to thousands of gold seekers. Most of them found little except misery and debt.

Mining camps sprang up wherever enough people gathered to look for gold. Among the gold seekers were thousands of immigrants from Mexico, China, Europe, and South America. Many found that they could earn a living by supplying miners with basic services like cooking, washing clothes, operating boardinghouses, or even providing legal services. Biddy Mason and her family, slaves brought to California by a forty-niner from Georgia, gained their freedom and managed to buy some land near the village of Los Angeles. Soon Mason became one of the weathiest landowners in California.

> **Who had more "job security," the miners or the service providers? Why?**
> _____
> _____
> _____
> _____

IMPACT ON CALIFORNIA

The forty-niners brought a population explosion and an economic boom to California. It became the 31st state of the Union in 1850. As the gold rush faded, many Californians took to farming and ranching. However, California remained isolated from the rest of the country until the transcontinental railroad was completed in 1869.

> **What consequence of the gold rush made California eligible for statehood?**
> _____
> _____

CHALLENGE ACTIVITY

Critical Thinking: Drawing Inferences Design and write a brochure inviting easterners to come to Sutter's colony in California and start a new life.

Copyright © by Holt, Rinehart and Winston. All rights reserved.

The North

CHAPTER SUMMARY

The Industrial Revolution		The Transportation Revolution
Caused by		Caused by
↓		↓
invention of machines		invention of the railroad
_____		_____
led to		led to
↓		↓
_____		_____
_____		_____

COMPREHENSION AND CRITICAL THINKING

As you read the section summaries, fill in the blanks above and answer the questions below.

1. Comparing Compare one cause of the Industrial Revolution with one cause of the Transportation Revolution.

_____

_____

2. Identify Cause and Effect Name two ways in which the Industrial Revolution changed the lives of the American people.

_____

_____

_____

3. Identify Cause and Effect Name two ways in which the Transportation Revolution changed the lives of the American people.

_____

_____

_____

Copyright © by Holt, Rinehart and Winston. All rights reserved.

The North

MAIN IDEAS

1. The invention of new machines in Great Britain led to the beginning of the Industrial Revolution.

2. The development of new machines and processes brought the Industrial Revolution to the United States.

3. Despite a slow start in manufacturing, the United States made rapid improvements during the War of 1812.

Key Terms and People

Industrial Revolution a period of rapid growth in the use of machines in manufacturing and production

textiles cloth items

Richard Arkwright an inventor who patented a large spinning machine, called the water frame, that ran on water power and created dozens of cotton threads at once

Samuel Slater a skilled British mechanic who could build the new textile machines

technology the tools used to produce items or to do work

Eli Whitney an inventor with an idea for mass-producing guns

interchangeable parts pieces that are exactly the same

mass production the efficient production of large numbers of identical goods

Academic Vocabulary

efficient productive and not wasteful

Section Summary

THE INDUSTRIAL REVOLUTION

In the early 1700s, most people in the United States and Europe made a living by farming. Female family members often used hand tools to make cloth for families. The sale of extra cloth earned money. Skilled workers such as blacksmiths set up shops to earn money by manufacturing goods by hand.

The **Industrial Revolution** would completely change that way of life. By the mid-1700s, cities and populations had grown. Demand increased for **efficient** and faster ways to make items.

> **In what way were goods made in the early 1700s?**
>
> _____
> _____
> _____

Copyright © by Holt, Rinehart and Winston. All rights reserved.

Section 1, *continued*

Textiles provided the first breakthrough. **Richard Arkwright** invented a machine that lowered the cost of cotton cloth and raised production speed. The machine was large and needed a power source. Most textile mills were built near streams to use running water for power.

> **In what way did Arkwright's machine make history?**
> _____
> _____

NEW MACHINES AND PROCESSES

Samuel Slater knew how to build machines that were used in Britain to make cloth more efficiently. He emigrated to the United States, and with Moses Brown opened a mill in Pawtucket, Rhode Island. The mill made cotton thread by machine. It was a success. Most mills were in the northeast, the region with many rivers and streams for power.

> **What information did Slater bring with him to the United States?**
> _____
> _____

In the 1790s U.S. gun makers could not produce muskets quickly enough to satisfy the government's demand. Better **technology** was needed. **Eli Whitney** had the idea of manufacturing using **interchangeable parts**. Whitney assembled muskets for President Adams. His idea worked. **Mass production** was soon used in factories making interchangeable parts.

> **What was Whitney's revolutionary idea?**
> _____
> _____
> _____

MANUFACTURING GROWS SLOWLY

U.S. manufacturing spread slowly. People who could buy good farmland would not work for low factory wages. British goods were cheaper than American goods. However, during the War of 1812 many Americans learned that they had relied on foreign goods too much. In 1815 the war ended and free trade returned. Businesspeople wanted to lead the nation into a time of industrial growth.

> **Why had Americans relied on foreign goods too much?**
> _____
> _____

CHALLENGE ACTIVITY

Critical Thinking: Rating In comparing the three inventors in Section 1, rate them from 1 to 3. Defend your rating order in a brief essay.

Copyright © by Holt, Rinehart and Winston. All rights reserved.

Interactive Reader and Study Guide

The North

Section 2

MAIN IDEAS

1. The spread of mills in the Northeast changed workers' lives.
2. The Lowell system revolutionized the textile industry in the Northeast.
3. Workers organized to reform working conditions

Key Terms and People

Rhode Island system Samuel Slater's strategy of hiring families and dividing factory work into simple tasks

Francis Cabot Lowell a New England businessman who built a loom that could both weave thread and spin cloth in the same mill

Lowell system Lowell's practice of hiring young unmarried women to work in his mills

trade unions groups of skilled workers that tried to improve members' pay and working conditions

strikes union workers' refusal to work until their employers met their demands

Sarah G. Bagley a mill worker who founded the Lowell Female Labor Reform Association

Academic Vocabulary

concrete specific, real

Section Summary

MILLS CHANGE WORKERS' LIVES

Samuel Slater had difficulty hiring enough people to work in his mills. Young male apprentices often left because their work was boring. Slater began hiring entire families to move to Pawtucket.

Slater constructed housing for the workers. He paid workers in credit at the company store rather than paying them cash. This way Slater could reinvest money in his business. Children usually earned in one week what an adult was paid for one day's work. Slater's method was known as the **Rhode Island system**. Many northeastern mill owners imitated Slater's system.

How much did child workers earn in factories?

_____

_____

Copyright © by Holt, Rinehart and Winston. All rights reserved.

Section 2, *continued*

THE LOWELL SYSTEM

Francis Cabot Lowell developed a different approach called the **Lowell system**. It transformed the Northeast's textile industry. With the aid of a company, Lowell built mills in Waltham and Lowell, both in Massachusetts. The factories were clean, and the workers' boardinghouses were neat.

Many young women, called Lowell girls, journeyed from across New England to earn money instead of earning nothing on the family farm. The Lowell girls were encouraged to take classes and join clubs. However, they worked 12- to 14-hour days, and cotton dust caused health problems for them.

> Name one advantage and one disadvantage of Lowell mill work.
> _____
> _____
> _____

WORKERS ORGANIZE

Factory workers' wages went down as people competed for jobs. Immigrants also competed for jobs. The Panic of 1837 led to unemployment for many. Skilled workers started **trade unions** for protection. Sometimes union members held **strikes**. But most strikes were not very successful.

Sarah G. Bagley battled for the workers. She was the first highly ranked woman in America's labor movement. In 1840 President Martin Van Buren had given a 10-hour workday to many federal employees. Bagley wanted the 10-hour workday for all workers.

> Why did workers' pay decrease?
> _____
> _____

The Unions won some **concrete** legal victories. Some states passed 10-hour workday laws. But companies often found ways to get around them. Other states did not pass the 10-hour workday laws. Union supporters kept fighting for improved working conditions during the 1800s.

> What did workers achieve in the mid-1800s?
> _____
> _____

CHALLENGE ACTIVITY

Critical Thinking: Contrasting Write a letter to the editor contrasting the lives of workers in Slater's mills and Lowell's mills.

Copyright © by Holt, Rinehart and Winston. All rights reserved.

The North

MAIN IDEAS

1. The Transportation Revolution affected trade and daily life.
2. The steamboat was one of the first developments of the Transportation Revolution.
3. Railroads were a vital part of the Transportation Revolution.
4. The Transportation Revolution brought many changes to American life and industry.

Key Terms and People

Transportation Revolution a period of rapid growth in the speed and convenience of travel

Robert Fulton an American who had the first full-time commercial steamboat in the United States

Clermont a steamboat that could travel up the Hudson River with no trouble

Gibbons* v. *Ogden the first U.S. Supreme Court ruling on commerce between states

Peter Cooper an American who built the *Tom Thumb,* a small steam train with great power and speed

Section Summary

TRADE AND DAILY LIFE

Along with the Industrial Revolution, the **Transportation Revolution** changed life in the 1800s by speeding travel and decreasing cost of shipping goods. People and information began traveling at much higher speeds. New towns and businesses sprang up with improved communication, travel, and trade. The steamboat and the railroad, new kinds of transportation, quickened the pace of American life.

> **Why did information begin traveling at higher speeds?**
> _____
> _____
> _____

> **In what way might the pace of American life have increased?**
> _____
> _____
> _____

STEAMBOATS

In the late 1700s American and European inventors advanced steam-powered boats. **Robert Fulton** tested the ***Clermont*** in the United States. The successful test helped launch the steamboat era.

Copyright © by Holt, Rinehart and Winston. All rights reserved.

Interactive Reader and Study Guide

Section 3, continued

Steamboats cut months off the time needed to travel from one place to another. They made trips up rivers cheaper and easier. Shipping goods from East to West, West to East, or overseas also was easier.

Sometimes the changes in transportation led to legal conflicts. In a landmark case, *Gibbons* v. *Ogden*, the court ruled that federal shipping laws overruled state shipping laws.

> How did steamboats affect shipping?
> _____
> _____

AMERICAN RAILROADS

In 1830 **Peter Cooper** built the *Tom Thumb*, a small but fast train. Excitement over rail travel grew in the mid-1800s. By 1860 about 30,000 miles of railroad tracks joined nearly every major eastern U.S. city. Trains took goods to faraway markets. Train travel averaged about 20 miles per hour and could be dangerous because of fires and derailment. But the dangers did not discourage travelers who wanted to go places faster.

> Circle the sentence that explains why travelers put up with the dangers of railroad travel.

TRANSPORTATION REVOLUTION BRINGS CHANGES

Trains brought new residents and raw materials for industry to cities, spurring growth. Coal replaced wood as a source of fuel because of its greater efficiency. That led to growth in the mining industry. Steel was used for railroad tracks, so the demand for steel increased. Railroad transportation also helped logging expand because wood was needed to build new houses in the growing cities. Chicago, on Lake Michigan, became a hub for national transportation.

> What helped the steel industry?
> _____

CHALLENGE ACTIVITY

Critical Thinking: Designing Design a four-page brochure advertising the wonders of travel by steamboat or train.

Copyright © by Holt, Rinehart and Winston. All rights reserved.

Interactive Reader and Study Guide

The North

MAIN IDEAS

1. The telegraph made swift communication possible from coast to coast.
2. With the shift to steam power, businesses built new factories closer to cities and transportation centers.
3. Improved farm equipment and other labor-saving devices made life easier for many Americans.
4. New inventions changed lives in American homes.

Key Terms and People

Samuel F. B. Morse the inventor of the telegraph

telegraph a device that could send information over wires across great distances

Morse code a system in which dots and dashes are used to stand for each letter of the alphabet

John Deere a blacksmith who first used the steel plow design

Cyrus McCormick the developer of a new harvesting machine called a mechanical reaper

Isaac Singer an inventor who made improvements in the design of the sewing machine

Section Summary

TELEGRAPH SPEEDS COMMUNICATION

Samuel F. B. Morse invented the **telegraph** in 1832. Morse used the work of two other scientists in making this practical machine. Telegraphs carry pulses, or surges, of electric current over wires. The operator touches a bar, called a telegraph key, that sets the length of each pulse. At the wire's other end, the pulses change into clicks. A short click is a dot; a long click is a dash.

Morse's assistant, Alfred Lewis Vail, developed the **Morse code**. Some people did not think Morse could actually read messages sent across long distances. But during the 1844 Democratic Convention in Baltimore, Maryland, a telegraph wired news of a nomination to politicians who were in Washington. Soon telegraphs were relaying messages for

> What was the invention of the telegraph based on?
> _____
> _____

> Did everyone accept the telegraph's power at first?
> _____
> _____

Copyright © by Holt, Rinehart and Winston. All rights reserved.

Interactive Reader and Study Guide

businesses, the government, newspapers, and private citizens. Telegraph lines were strung on poles next to railroad tracks across the country.

Why did telegraph messages become so widely used?

_____

_____

_____

STEAM POWER AND NEW FACTORIES

Most factories, operating on water power at first, had to be built near water. With the use of steam engines, factories could be built almost anywhere. Still, most were in the Northeast. By 1860 New England had as many factories as all of the South had. Many new factories were near cities and transportation centers, giving them better access to workers. In addition, by the 1840s new machinery could produce interchangeable parts.

Why could newer factories be built almost anywhere?

_____

_____

_____

IMPROVED FARM EQUIPMENT

John Deere was selling 1,000 steel plows a year by 1846. **Cyrus McCormick** mass-produced his reapers in a large Chicago factory. His company advertised, provided service, and let customers buy on credit. The plow and the reaper allowed Midwestern farmers to harvest huge wheat fields.

Circle the sentence that explains what new methods McCormick used to persuade people to buy his reapers.

CHANGING LIFE AT HOME

The sewing machine was among the American inventions that made home life easier. **Isaac Singer** modified the sewing machine and worked hard to sell his product. Prices of many household items had decreased, giving many more people the ability to afford them.

Why did the purchase of many household items increase?

_____

_____

_____

CHALLENGE ACTIVITY

Critical Thinking: Evaluating Write a brief essay explaining which invention mentioned in this section made the biggest change in people's lives.

Copyright © by Holt, Rinehart and Winston. All rights reserved.

Interactive Reader and Study Guide

The South

CHAPTER SUMMARY

CAUSE		EFFECT
The price of cash crops drops.	⟶	The need for slaves decreases.
Eli Whitney's cotton gin makes it profitable to grow cotton.	⟶	
	⟶	Most Southerners own few or no slaves.
Slave behavior is strictly controlled.	⟶	Slaves create their own culture, and some rebel.

COMPREHENSION AND CRITICAL THINKING

As you read the section summaries, complete the table above and answer the questions below.

1. Draw Conclusions How did Whitney's cotton gin affect the value of slaves?

_____

_____

_____

_____

2. Identify Cause and Effect Why did only one-third of southerners own slaves?

_____

_____

_____

_____

3. Make Judgments Do you think there was a time when southern farmers depended on cash crops? Why or why not?

_____

_____

_____

_____

Copyright © by Holt, Rinehart and Winston. All rights reserved.

The South

MAIN IDEAS

1. The invention of the cotton gin revived the economy of the South.
2. The cotton gin created a cotton boom in which farmers grew little else.
3. Some people encouraged southerners to focus on other crops and industries.

Key Terms and People

cotton gin machine that separates cotton from its seeds

planters large-scale farmers who owned more than 20 slaves

cotton belt nickname for the region that grew most of the country's cotton crop

factors crop brokers who arranged transportation of goods aboard trading ships

Tredegar Iron Works in its day, the only large southern factory that made iron products

Academic Vocabulary

primary main, most important

Section Summary

REVIVING THE SOUTH'S ECONOMY

After the American Revolution, the use of slaves began to decline. Because crop prices fell, farmers planted less, so they needed less slave labor.

Cotton was not a new crop to the southern states. However, few farmers planted much, for the short-staple cotton that grew well there was very hard to separate from its seeds. Northerner Eli Whitney changed that when he invented the **cotton gin**.

This hand-cranked cylinder easily pulled cotton and seeds apart. With the cotton gin, cotton crops became profitable. A cotton gin could clean as much cotton as planters could plant and their slaves could pick. A **planter** was a large-scale farmer who owned more than 20 slaves.

> Why was it difficult to harvest cotton before the invention of the cotton gin?
>
> _____
>
> _____

Copyright © by Holt, Rinehart and Winston. All rights reserved.

Interactive Reader and Study Guide

THE COTTON BOOM

For southern farmers cotton had many advantages over other crops. Unlike food products cotton could be stored for long periods of time. Plus its lightness made it fairly inexpensive to transport. As a result, the cotton-supported slave trade grew, even as Congress worked to limit slavery in the nation.

What were the advantages of cotton compared to other crops?

_____

_____

Most of the country's cotton was produced in the **cotton belt**, which stretched from South Carolina to Texas. Without transportation systems such as roads and canals, southern farmers relied on rivers to move their cotton. When the cotton reached a port, the farmers sold their cotton to merchants who then contacted **factors** to arrange transportation for the cotton aboard trading ships.

Why were the region's rivers especially important to southern farmers?

_____

_____

OTHER CROPS AND INDUSTRIES

Scientific agriculture, or the use of scientific methods to improve farmng, encouraged southern farmers to rotate the kinds of crops they planted. The **primary** food crop of the South was corn, but farmers also grew rice, sugarcane, wheat, tobacco, hemp, and flax. Some southerners encouraged the growth of industry. As a result, some industries, such as the **Tredegar Iron Works**, also flourished. Still, most of the South focused on farming.

Circle the definition of scientific agriculture.

CHALLENGE ACTIVITY

Critical Thinking: Write to Explain What if a new fiber was discovered that replaced cotton in clothing? What effect would this development have on cotton planters? Write a paragraph explaining how falling cotton prices might lead to less demand for farm workers.

Copyright © by Holt, Rinehart and Winston. All rights reserved.

The South

MAIN IDEAS

1. Southern society and culture consisted of four main groups.
2. Free African Americans in the South faced a great deal of discrimination.

Key Terms and People

yeomen owners of small farms

Section Summary

SOUTHERN SOCIETY AND CULTURE

Only about one-third of all southerners owned slaves. Far fewer were actually wealthy planters. However, those few planters were among the most influential southern citizens, and many were political leaders.

On the vast plantations, the planter ran the farm business. A wealthy planter would have overseers to help him. The planter's wife ran the household, which included many house slaves. She also was in charge of important social events such as dances and dinners.

Most southern farmers were yeomen. **Yeomen** owned small farms averaging about 100 acres, and often they worked side by side with the few slaves they might own.

Many white southerners were poor. They owned no slaves at all. Often they lived on land that could not grow crops. These farmers were at the bottom of the economic ladder.

Religion was central to southern life. One reason was its social impact. Often farm families only saw their neighbors at church functions. Some southerners also believed that Christianity justified slavery—a belief not shared by Christians in the North.

The economy of the South also depended on the businesses conducted in its busy cities. As in northern cities, southern cities provided many ser-

> **How was a yeoman different from a planter?**
> _____
> _____
> _____

> **Why was religion central to southern life?**
> _____
> _____
> _____

Copyright © by Holt, Rinehart and Winston. All rights reserved.

vices to residents, including water systems and street maintenance. Southern cities used slave labor, too. Businesses either owned slaves or hired them out from nearby planters.

FREE AFRICAN AMERICANS AND DISCRIMINATION

Not all African Americans were slaves. Some were free. Some had been born free. Others had bought their freedom from their slaveowners or had run away. About half of these free African Americans lived in the South.

The presence of free African Americans concerned some white southerners. They worried that those who were free would incite those who were enslaved to rise up against their owners. As a result, southern cities and states passed laws aimed at limiting the rights of these free African Americans.

Free African Americans posed a threat to the institution of slavery. Many whites believed the African American could not survive outside of slavery. They used this as justification for slavery. The free African Americans could prove this theory wrong.

> **How were southern cities like northern cities?**
> _____
> _____
> _____

> **Circle the sentence describing how many of the free African Americans lived in the South.**

> **According to many southerners, how did free African Americans threaten the South's slave system?**
> _____
> _____
> _____

CHALLENGE ACTIVITY

Critical Thinking: Evaluate How effective were the laws limiting the rights of free African Americans? Write five questions that could be answered by historical study and outline research that could help you answer your questions.

Copyright © by Holt, Rinehart and Winston. All rights reserved.

> **MAIN IDEAS**
> 1. Slaves worked at a variety of jobs on plantations.
> 2. Life under slavery was difficult and dehumanizing.
> 3. Slave culture centered around family, community, and religion.
> 4. Slave uprisings led to stricter slave codes in many states.

Key Terms and People

folktales stories with a moral

spirituals songs that combine African and European music and religious beliefs

Nat Turner's Rebellion the name given to the 1831 rebellion led by Nat Turner

Nat Turner Virginia slave who led a rebellion against slaveholders in 1831

Academic Vocabulary

aspect part

Section Summary

SLAVES AND WORK

Most planters used the gang labor system to get their fields farmed. In this system enslaved men, women, and children over 10 years of age all did the same fieldwork from dawn until dark.

Slaves with special skills often were rented out by their owners. Sometimes these slaves were allowed to keep part of what they earned. As a consequence, some skilled slaves were able to save enough money to buy their own freedom.

> **How could skilled slaves buy their freedom?**
> _____
> _____
> _____

LIFE UNDER SLAVERY

To most southern slaveholders, slaves were property, not people. As property, slaves could be bought and sold. Usually, this business occurred at a slave auction. At these auctions family members could be sold away from each other forever.

> **What could happen to family members at a slave auction?**
> _____
> _____

Copyright © by Holt, Rinehart and Winston. All rights reserved.

Section 3, *continued*

Many slaveholders used cruel punishments to make sure their slaves stayed obedient. In addition, many states passed strict slave codes. These laws limited what slaves could do. For example, in some states it was illegal to teach slaves to read and write.

> How were laws used to control slaves?
> _____
> _____
> _____

SLAVE CULTURE

For enslaved African Americans, the family was the most important **aspect** of their lives. Parents made sure their children knew the African part of their history, including African customs and traditions. Since they could not read and write, they passed this information verbally. Some of their stories were **folktales**—stories with morals—to teach children how to survive slavery.

> How did slaves keep their culture alive?
> _____
> _____
> _____

Religion was also an important part of the culture of enslaved African Americans. Christian slaves believed that, in God's eyes, they were equal to anyone else. They held onto the hope that someday they would be freed. Often, these beliefs were expressed in the **spirituals** they sang.

SLAVE UPRISINGS

Enslaved African Americans found a variety of ways to protest their treatment. Some even ran away. But getting all the way North to freedom was filled with dangers and hardships. Most runaways were caught and forced to return.

Sometimes, slaves protested with violence. They risked certain punishment. This was true of Virginia slave **Nat Turner**. During **Nat Turner's Rebellion** in 1831, slaves killed about 60 white people. In the end, though, more that 100 slaves were killed, and Turner was executed. As a result, many states strengthened their slave codes.

> When did Nat Turner's Rebellion occur?
> _____
> _____

CHALLENGE ACTIVITY

Critical Thinking: Analyze Write a paragraph explaining why southern slaveholders would want to keep slaves from learning to read and write.

Copyright © by Holt, Rinehart and Winston. All rights reserved.

Interactive Reader and Study Guide

New Movements in America

CHAPTER SUMMARY

	THEN . . .	Nativists start to worry about their job security.
The philosophy of transcendentalism becomes popular.	THEN . . .	Many American writers are influenced by these new beliefs.
The Second Great Awakening begins.	THEN . . .	
Many Americans believe slavery should end.	THEN . . .	The Underground Railroad helps slaves escape from the South.
	THEN . . .	

COMPREHENSION AND CRITICAL THINKING

As you read the section summaries, complete the table above and answer the questions below.

1. Explain What made nativists worry about their job security?

_____

_____

_____

2. Identify Sequence What reforms followed the Second Great Awakening?

_____

_____

_____

3. Draw a Conclusion What helped start the women's rights movement?

_____

_____

_____

Copyright © by Holt, Rinehart and Winston. All rights reserved.

Interactive Reader and Study Guide

Name _____ Class _____ Date _____

Section 1

> **MAIN IDEAS**
> 1. Millions of immigrants, mostly German and Irish, arrived in the United States despite anti-immigrant movements.
> 2. Industrialization led to the growth of cities.
> 3. American cities experienced urban problems due to rapid growth.

Key Terms and People

nativists people who opposed immigration

Know-Nothing Party political organization founded by nativists in 1849

middle class a social and economic level between the wealthy and the poor

tenements dirty, unsafe housing structures in which the cities' poor were forced to live

Academic Vocabulary

implicit understood though not clearly put into words

Section Summary

MILLIONS OF IMMIGRANTS ARRIVE

Between 1840 and 1860, more than four million immigrants came to the United States. Many came from Ireland, fleeing starvation that came with a terrible potato famine there. The famine also meant that many Irish immigrants arrived poor. These immigrants often got jobs working long hours for little pay.

Unlike the Irish, immigrants from Germany often arrived with some money. Many came to America after a revolution in their homeland. Others came for the opportunities America offered. Many bought farmland in America's Midwest. Others settled and worked in cities.

To many native-born Americans, the new immigrants posed an **implicit** threat. Americans worried that immigrants would take away their jobs. Immigrants would do the same work but for less money. The Americans also mistrusted immigrants

> Compare and contrast Irish and German immigration between 1840 and 1860.
> _____
> _____
> _____

> Why did nativists worry about the increasing numbers of immigrants?
> _____
> _____

Copyright © by Holt, Rinehart and Winston. All rights reserved.

who were Catholic. In Europe, Protestants and
Catholics had a history of conflicts.

Americans who opposed immigration for these
reasons were known as **nativists**. Together, the
nativists formed a political group called the **Know-
Nothing Party**, which tried to limit immigration.

RAPID GROWTH OF CITIES

In the mid-1800s, the Industrial Revolution encouraged rapid growth in America's cities. The jobs the
Industrial Revolution created also helped build a
middle class—a social and economic level between
the wealthy and the poor. These new urban dwell-
ers enjoyed the culture in America's cities. Libraries,
clubs, and theaters grew as the cities grew.

> Why do you think culture changed
> after the Industrial Revolution?
> _____
> _____

URBAN PROBLEMS

The people who moved to the city to work could
afford only tenement rents. **Tenements** were poorly
designed housing structures that were dirty, overcrowded, and unsafe. Cities had not yet learned how
to deal with the filth and garbage generated by so
many people, and killer epidemics resulted. Crime
and fires also plagued the fast-growing cities of the
United States.

> Why were living conditions so
> poor in urban areas?
> _____
> _____

CHALLENGE ACTIVITY

Critical Thinking: Summarize List some of the health and safety issues
that plagued America's cities during the first half of the 1800s.

Copyright © by Holt, Rinehart and Winston. All rights reserved.

New Movements in America

Section 2

MAIN IDEAS

1. Transcendentalists and utopian communities withdrew from American society.
2. American Romantic painters and writers made important contributions to art and literature.

Key Terms and People

transcendentalism belief that people should rise above material things in life and that people should depend on themselves rather than outside authority

Ralph Waldo Emerson American writer most famous for his essay "Self-Reliance"

Margaret Fuller American writer who wrote and edited material on transcendentism

Henry David Thoreau American writer most famous for the transcendental ideas he summarized in his book *Walden*

utopian communities experimental communities that tried to create a perfect society

Nathaniel Hawthorne American writer best known for his novel *The Scarlet Letter*

Edgar Allan Poe American writer best known for his short stories and poetry

Emily Dickinson American poet whose short-style poems were published after her death

Henry Wadsworth Longfellow American poet who wrote popular story-poems like *The Song of Hiawatha*

Walt Whitman American poet best known for his poem *Leaves of Grass*

Academic Vocabulary

abstract expressing an idea without reference to an actual thing

Section Summary

TRANSCENDENTALISTS

Transcendentalism was a belief system in which followers thought they could rise above the material things in life. Transcendentalists believed that people should depend on themselves rather than outside authority. **Ralph Waldo Emerson, Margaret Fuller,** and **Henry David Thoreau** were among the great American thinkers who were also transcendentalists.

Emerson expressed his ideas in the essay "Self-Reliance." Fuller wrote *Women in the Nineteenth Century,* a book about women's basic rights. In his

> Name two transcendentalist thinkers.
>
> _____
>
> _____

Copyright © by Holt, Rinehart and Winston. All rights reserved.

Section 2, *continued*

book *Life in the Woods*, Thoreau summarized many
of his transcendentalist beliefs.

Some transcendentalists created communities
apart from society. In these **utopian communities**,
people hoped to form a perfect society. Some, such
as the Shaker communities, were based on religious
beliefs. Other groups pursued utopian lifestyles for
abstract and transcendental reasons.

> Why might transcendentalists seek
> to create utopian communities?
> _____
> _____
> _____

AMERICAN ROMANTICISM

In the early and mid-1800s, many artists were
inspired by simple life and nature's beauty. Some
joined the Romantic movement that began in
Europe with British poets such as Blake, Byron,
Keats, and Shelley. For the Romantics, each person
brought a unique point of view to the world. These
writers used their emotions to guide their words.

At this time American Romantic writers began
to develop an American style. Female writers such
as Ann Sophia Stephens wrote popular historical
fiction. Another historical novel, *The Scarlet Letter*
by **Nathaniel Hawthorne**, described Puritan life in
America. Herman Melville wrote *Moby Dick*, considered to be one of America's finest novels. **Edgar
Allan Poe** also gained fame for his short stories and
poetry.

> Underline all the writers' names
> that appear in this section. Put an
> 'X' by the names you have heard
> before.

Emily Dickinson, **Henry Wadsworth
Longfellow**, and John Greenleaf Whittier are just
three poets of this time whose works have long out-
lived them. The same is true of **Walt Whitman**, who
used his collection of poems *Leaves of Grass* to praise
American individualism and democracy.

> Circle the titles of famous novels
> written by American Romantics.

CHALLENGE ACTIVITY

Critical Thinking: Make Inferences In this section certain writers'
names appear in bold print while other names do not. Explain what you
think the difference is. Why is it important to notice the difference?

Copyright © by Holt, Rinehart and Winston. All rights reserved.

New Movements in America

MAIN IDEAS

1. The Second Great Awakening sparked interest in religion.

2. Social reformers began to speak out about temperance and prison reform.

3. Improvements in education reform affected many parts of the population.

4. Northern African American communities became involved in reform efforts.

Key Terms and People

Second Great Awakening late 1700s-early 1800s movement of Christian renewal

Charles Grandison Finney minister who challenged some traditional beliefs

temperance movement movement to encourage people not to drink alcohol

Lyman Beecher minister who spoke against both Charles Grandison Finney and alcohol consumption

Dorothea Dix prison reformer

common-school movement movement to have all children, regardless of background, taught in a common place

Horace Mann education reformer

Catherine Beecher founder of all-female academy in Hartford, Connecticut

Thomas Gallaudet education reformer for the hearing impaired

Section Summary

SECOND GREAT AWAKENING

During the 1790s, a period of Christian renew-al began. It was known as the **Second Great Awakening.** By the 1830s, it had swept through New England, the Appalachians, and the South.

Charles Grandison Finney was one of the leaders of the Second Great Awakening. Some, like Boston's Lyman Beecher, did not agree with Finney's message. However, the Constitution's First Amendment guaranteed Finney's right to speak and be heard. Through the efforts of Finney and other ministers, many Americans joined churches across the country.

> What can you infer from the fact that this period was called the Second Great Awakening?
> _____
> _____

SOCIAL REFORMERS SPEAK OUT

In the spirit of the Second Great Awakening, people tried to reform many of society's ills. In the **temper-**

Copyright © by Holt, Rinehart and Winston. All rights reserved.

ance movement, people aimed at limiting alcohol consumption. **Lyman Beecher** and other ministers spoke about the evils of alcohol.

Another reformer, **Dorothea Dix**, reported on the terrible conditions she found when she visited some Massachusetts prisons. Imprisoned along with adult criminals were the mentally ill and children. Because of efforts by Dix and others, governments built hospitals for the mentally ill and reform schools for young lawbreakers. They also began to try to reform—not just punish—prisoners.

> How did prisons change as a result of reformers like Dorothea Dix?
> _____
> _____
> _____

IMPROVEMENTS IN EDUCATION

Education in the early 1800s improved with the **common-school movement**. This movement, led by **Horace Mann**, worked to have all students, regardless of background, taught in the same place. Women's education also improved at this time. Several women's schools, including **Catherine Beecher's** all-female academy in Connecticut, opened. Teaching people with disabilities improved, too. For example, **Thomas Gallaudet** bettered the education of the hearing impaired.

> What was the common-school movement?
> _____
> _____

AFRICAN AMERICAN COMMUNITIES

In this period, life improved for the nation's free black population. The Free Africans Religious Society, founded by Richard Allen, pressed for equality and education. Leaders such as Alexander Crummel helped build African American schools in New York, Philadelphia, and other cities. In 1835 Oberlin College became the first college to admit African Americans. Soon after, in the 1840s, several African American colleges were founded.

> Circle the names of all the reformers who worked to better America during this time.

CHALLENGE ACTIVITY

Critical Thinking: Compare and Contrast What did Horace Mann, Catherine Beecher, Thomas Gallaudet, and Richard Allen all have in common?

Copyright © by Holt, Rinehart and Winston. All rights reserved.

New Movements in America

MAIN IDEAS

1. Americans from a variety of backgrounds actively opposed slavery.

2. Abolitionists organized the Underground Railroad to help enslaved Africans escape.

3. Despite efforts of abolitionists, many Americans remained opposed to ending slavery.

Key Terms and People

abolition complete end to slavery

William Lloyd Garrison abolitionist who ran the *Liberator* newspaper and also helped found the American Anti-Slavery Society

American Anti-Slavery Society organization that wanted immediate emancipation and racial equality

Angelina and Sarah Grimké southern sisters who spoke in favor of abolition

Frederick Douglass ex-slave who became a pro-abolition speaker

Sojourner Truth ex-slave who spoke for abolition and women's rights

Underground Railroad loosely organized group that helped slaves escape from the South

Harriet Tubman ex-slave who freed more than 300 others using the Underground Railroad

Section Summary

AMERICANS OPPOSE SLAVERY

By the 1830s, many Americans formed a movement to end slavery. They supported **abolition**. These abolitionists worked for emancipation, or freedom from slavery, for all who lived in the United States.

Some abolitionists thought that ex-slaves should get the same rights enjoyed by other Americans. Others, however, hoped to send the freed blacks back to Africa to start new colonies there. In fact, the American Colonization Society successfully founded the African colony of Liberia.

Many abolitionists spread the message of abolition using the power of the pen. **William Lloyd**

> What is the difference between abolition and emancipation?
>
> _____
>
> _____
>
> _____

Copyright © by Holt, Rinehart and Winston. All rights reserved.

Garrison, for example, ran the *Liberator* newspaper. He also helped found the **American Anti-Slavery Society**. This group believed in emancipation and racial equality. **Angelina and Sarah Grimké** were two sisters from a southern slave-holding family. They wrote pamphlets and a book to try to convince other white people to join the fight against slavery.

When **Frederick Douglass** was a slave, he secretly learned to read and write. After he escaped slavery, he used those skills to support the abolition movement by publishing a newspaper and writing books about his life. Douglass also was a powerful speaker who vividly described slavery's horrors. Many other ex-slaves also were active abolitionists. One example was **Sojourner Truth**, who became famous for her anti-slavery speeches.

> Why do you think Frederick Douglass had to learn to read and write in secret?
> _____
> _____
> _____

> How were the intended audiences different for the Grimké sisters and Sojourner Truth?
> _____
> _____
> _____

THE UNDERGROUND RAILROAD

The **Underground Railroad** was the name given a loosely knit group of white and black abolitionists who held escaped slaves get North to freedom. One of the most famous "conductors" on this Railroad was an ex-slave named **Harriet Tubman**. She made 19 trips to the north, freeing more than 300 slaves.

> What do you think would happen to someone who was caught helping slaves escape?
> _____
> _____
> _____

OPPOSITION TO ENDING SLAVERY

Many white southerners felt slavery was vital to their economy. They also felt that outsiders should not tell them what to do. Some justified enslaving people by claiming that African Americans needed the structure of slavery to survive.

CHALLENGE ACTIVITY

Critical Thinking: Make Inferences Why do you think Frederick Douglass called his newspaper the *North Star?*

Copyright © by Holt, Rinehart and Winston. All rights reserved.

New Movements in America

MAIN IDEAS

1. Influenced by the abolition movement, many women struggled to gain equal rights for themselves.

2. Calls for women's rights met opposition from men and women.

3. The Seneca Falls Convention launched the first organized women's rights movement in the United States.

Key Terms and People

Elizabeth Cady Stanton supporter of women's rights who helped organize the Seneca Falls Convention

Lucretia Mott women's rights supporter who helped organize the Seneca Falls Convention

Seneca Falls Convention the first organized public meeting about women's rights held in the United States

Declaration of Sentiments the document officially requesting equal rights for women

Lucy Stone spokesperson for the Anti-Slavery Society and the women's rights movement

Susan B. Anthony women's rights supporter who argued for equal pay for equal work, the right of women to enter traditionally male professions, and property rights

Section Summary

WOMEN'S STRUGGLE FOR EQUAL RIGHTS

In the mid-1800s, some female abolitionists also began to focus on the women's rights in America, despite their many critics. For example, the Grimké sisters were criticized for speaking in public. Their critics felt they should stay at home. Sarah Grimké responded by writing a pamphlet in support of women's rights. She also argued for equal educational opportunities, as well as for laws that treated women in an equal manner.

Abolitionist Sojourner Truth also became a women's-rights supporter. The ex-slave never learned to read or write, but she became a great and influential speaker.

> Why did critics of the Grimké sisters think women should not speak in public?
>
> _____
>
> _____

Copyright © by Holt, Rinehart and Winston. All rights reserved.

OPPOSING THE CALL FOR WOMEN'S RIGHTS

The women's movement had many critics—both men and women. Some felt a woman should stay home. Others felt women were not as physically or mentally strong as men. Therefore, they needed the protection of first their fathers, then their husbands. This was why upon marriage, husbands took control of their wives' property.

> What did the abolition and women's rights movements have in common?
>
> _____
>
> _____

SENECA FALLS CONVENTION

With the support of leaders like **Elizabeth Cady Stanton** and **Lucretia Mott**, the **Seneca Falls Convention** opened July 19, 1848, in Seneca Falls, New York. It was the first time American women organized to promote women's rights. It resulted in the **Declaration of Sentiments**. This document officially requested equality for women. It brought 18 charges against men, much as the Declaration of Independence had brought 18 charges against King George III.

> What were some of the rights for which women were fighting?
>
> _____
>
> _____

After the convention, more women rose to lead the fight for rights. **Lucy Stone**, for example, was another abolitionist who spoke out for women's rights. So did **Susan B. Anthony**. Anthony argued that women should be paid the same as men for the same job, and that women could do the jobs reserved for men. Anthony also fought for property rights for women. Many states changed their property laws because of her efforts. But some rights, such as the right to vote, were not won until much later.

> Why do you think most of the leaders in the women's rights movement were women?
>
> _____
>
> _____
>
> _____

CHALLENGE ACTIVITY

Critical Thinking: Evaluate Identify the women you think had the greatest impact on women's rights. Write a sentence or two explaining your choice.

Copyright © by Holt, Rinehart and Winston. All rights reserved.

A Divided Nation

CHAPTER SUMMARY

Northern states fight slavery spreading west.

Kansas becomes a blood battlefield for pro-slavery and anti-slavery Americans.

The nation breaks in two.

COMPREHENSION AND CRITICAL THINKING

As you read the section summaries, complete the empty boxes above and answer the questions below.

1. Interpret Information What earned Kansas the nickname "Bleeding Kansas"?

_____

_____

_____

2. Draw Conclusions List two events involving Abraham Lincoln that led to the breakup of the nation.

_____

_____

_____

3. Make Inferences Why do you think Lincoln was against the spread of slavery? Explain your answer.

_____

_____

_____

_____

_____

Copyright © by Holt, Rinehart and Winston. All rights reserved.

A Divided Nation

MAIN IDEAS

1. The addition of new land in the West renewed disputes over the expansion of slavery.
2. The Compromise of 1850 tried to solve the disputes over slavery.
3. The Fugitive Slave Act caused more controversy.
4. Abolitionists used antislavery literature to promote opposition.

Key Terms and People

popular sovereignty the idea that political power belongs to the people

Wilmot Proviso suggested bill that would outlaw slavery in new U.S. territory

sectionalism situation in which people favor the interests of one region over those of the entire country

Free-Soil Party third political party that formed to support abolition

secede formally withdraw

Compromise of 1850 law that maintained America's slave-state/free-state balance

Fugitive Slave Act law that made it a crime to aid runaway slaves

Anthony Burns Virginia slave-fugitive whose attempted rescue from a Boston jail ended in violence

Uncle Tom's Cabin antislavery novel written by Harriet Beecher Stowe

Harriet Beecher Stowe author of the antislavery novel, *Uncle Tom's Cabin*

Section Summary

NEW LAND RENEWS SLAVERY DISPUTES

The nation's debate over slavery continued as the country got bigger. Many northerners for example, supported the **Wilmot Proviso**, which would outlaw slavery in new lands. Many southerners, on the other hand, did not support the bill. Arguments about the proviso showed how **sectionalism** was dividing the country.

Some favored the idea of **popular sovereignty**. They thought each region's voters should decide the question of slavery for that region. The debate was so intense that a third political party, the **Free-Soil Party,** formed to support abolition.

> **Why do you think southerners were opposed to the Wilmot Proviso?**
>
> _____
> _____
> _____

Copyright © by Holt, Rinehart and Winston. All rights reserved.

Interactive Reader and Study Guide

COMPROMISE OF 1850

The **Compromise of 1850** was presented by Kentucky's Senator Henry Clay. Its purpose was to maintain the delicate balance between slave and free states. It became law because of support by representatives like Senator Daniel Webster. Other lawmakers were not so happy. Senator John C. Calhoun of South Carolina asked that the slave states be allowed to **secede** from the Union.

> What made Henry Clay's law a compromise?
>
> _____
>
> _____
>
> _____

FUGITIVE SLAVE ACT

Part of the Compromise of 1850 required passage of the **Fugitive Slave Act**. This act made it a crime to help runaway slaves. Abolitionists especially reacted in anger to the Compromise. Sometimes that anger turned to violence. This was true when abolitionists tried to rescue Virginia fugitive **Anthony Burns** from a Boston jail.

> How can you tell that Anthony Burns was a slave?
>
> _____
>
> _____
>
> _____

ANTISLAVERY LITERATURE

Many abolitionists expressed their antislavery feelings in speeches. Others used the written word to influence people on the issue of slavery. One effective author was **Harriet Beecher Stowe**. In 1852 Stowe's antislavery novel, *Uncle Tom's Cabin*, was published. The book showed some of the consequences of slavery. It sold more than 2 million copies and influenced many to support the end of slavery.

> How did Harriet Beecher Stowe impact the issue of slavery in America?
>
> _____
>
> _____
>
> _____

CHALLENGE ACTIVITY

Critical Thinking: Write to Identify Write a paragraph about something you read or saw that made you change your mind. It could be a book, a speech, a television show—even a teacher.

Copyright © by Holt, Rinehart and Winston. All rights reserved.

A Divided Nation

MAIN IDEAS

1. The debate over the expansion of slavery influenced the election of 1852.

2. The Kansas-Nebraska Act allowed voters to allow or prohibit slavery.

3. Pro-slavery and antislavery groups clashed violently in what became known as "Bleeding Kansas."

Key Terms and People

Franklin Pierce Democratic candidate who won the presidential election of 1852

Stephen Douglas representative who introduced what would become the Kansas-Nebraska Act

Kansas-Nebraska Act the law that divided the rest of the Louisiana Purchase into two territories—Kansas and Nebraska

Pottawatomie Massacre the murder of five pro-slavery men at Pottawatomie Creek by John Brown and several other abolitionists

Charles Sumner Massachusetts senator who was an outspoken critic of pro-slavery leaders

Preston Brooks South Carolina representative who used a cane to beat Charles Sumner on the Senate floor for his criticisms of pro-slavery leaders

Academic Vocabulary

implications effects of a decision

Section Summary

ELECTION OF 1852

In the presidential election of 1852, the Democrats nominated **Franklin Pierce**. He was not a well-known politician, however his promise to honor the Compromise of 1850 assured him many southern votes. Pierce ran against Winfield Scott.

Pierce's win over Scott was resounding. When the votes were counted, it was discovered that out of the 31 states, 27 voted for Pierce.

> Why was Franklin Pierce a popular candidate in the South?
>
> _____
>
> _____

THE KANSAS-NEBRASKA ACT

The slavery issue continued to plague the United States. In 1854, Representative **Stephen Douglas**

Copyright © by Holt, Rinehart and Winston. All rights reserved.

Interactive Reader and Study Guide

introduced a bill that addressed slavery in the Louisiana Territory. When it was signed into law on May 30, it became known as the **Kansas-Nebraska Act**. It got its name from the two territories into which it divided the rest of Louisiana—Kansas and Nebraska. In each territory, popular sovereignty would determine the answer to the slavery question. Antislavery northerners feared the **implications** of the Act. They were afraid free territory would become slave territory.

> **How did the Kansas-Nebraska Act get its name?**
> _____
> _____
> _____

To make sure Kansas voted in favor of slavery, pro-slavery voters left their homes in Missouri to cross the border and vote in Kansas. They won and quickly set up a pro-slavery government. However those who did not believe in slavery set up another, separate government in Topeka.

> **What do you think would be the consequences of one state having two governments?**
> _____
> _____
> _____

BLEEDING KANSAS

In May 1856, pro-slavery jurors charged antislavery leaders with treason. Pro-slavery forces rode to Lawrence to arrest those charged. When they found the suspects had fled, they burned the town.

> **What caused the Sack of Lawrence?**
> _____
> _____
> _____
> _____
> _____

The Sack of Lawrence outraged many abolitionists, including New England abolitionist John Brown. Together with a small group that included four of his sons, Brown was responsible for the **Pottawatomie Massacre**, in which five pro-slavery men were killed. Quickly, Kansas fell into civil war.

Fighting even took place on the Senate floor. South Carolina Representative **Preston Brooks** used his cane to beat Massachusetts Senator **Charles Sumner** into unconsciousness because of Sumner's criticisms of pro-slavery leaders.

> **Was Senator Charles Sumner for or against slavery?**
> _____
> _____
> _____

CHALLENGE ACTIVITY

Critical Thinking: Write to Explain Write a few sentences to explain how Kansas got the nickname "Bleeding Kansas."

Copyright © by Holt, Rinehart and Winston. All rights reserved.

A Divided Nation

MAIN IDEAS

1. Political parties in the United States underwent change due to the movement to expand slavery.

2. The *Dred Scott* decision created further division over the issue of slavery.

3. The Lincoln-Douglas debates brought much attention to the conflict over slavery.

Key Terms and People

Republican Party political party founded to fight slavery

James Buchanan Democratic candidate and winner of the 1856 presidential election

John C. Frémont Republic candidate for the 1856 presidential election

Dred Scott slave who unsuccessfully sued for his freedom in 1846

Roger B. Taney Chief Justice of the Supreme Court during the *Dred Scott* decision

Abraham Lincoln early leader of the Republican Party

Lincoln-Douglas debates debates between senatorial candidates Abraham Lincoln and Stephen Douglas

Freeport Doctrine Stephen Douglas's belief in popular sovereignty, stated during the Freeport debate

Academic Vocabulary

complex difficult; not simple

Section Summary

POLITICAL PARTIES UNDERGO CHANGE

As the 1850s progressed Whigs, Democrats, Free-Soilers, and abolitionists united to create the **Republican Party** to fight slavery. Others left their parties to form the Know-Nothing Party. For the 1856 presidential election, the old Democratic Party nominated **James Buchanan**. Buchanan had been out of the country during the Kansas bloodshed, but he defeated Know-Nothing Millard Fillmore and Republican **John C. Frémont**.

> Why would it matter to voters that James Buchanan had been out of the country during "Bleeding Kansas"?
>
> _____
>
> _____
>
> _____

Copyright © by Holt, Rinehart and Winston. All rights reserved.

DRED SCOTT DECISION

Dred Scott was a slave. His slaveowner was a doc-
tor who traveled from Missouri, a slave state, to free
areas and back again to Missouri. Scott sued for his
freedom, since he had lived in free states.

The Supreme Court's decision in this **complex**
case was against Scott. Chief Justice **Roger B. Taney**
wrote that African Americans were not citizens, and
only citizens could sue in federal court. Taney also
wrote in the Dred Scott decision that slaves were
considered property, and Scott living in free territory did not make him free. Taney said that Congress
could not stop people from taking slaves into federal territory.

Many antislavery voices rose against the decision.
This included the voice of an Illinois lawyer named
Abraham Lincoln.

> Underline the three decisions the Supreme Court made in the *Dred Scott* case.

> Are you surprised to know that at the time of the *Dred Scott* decision, a majority of Supreme Court Justices were from the South? Why or why not?
>
> _____
> _____
> _____

LINCOLN-DOUGLAS DEBATES

In 1858 Abraham Lincoln ran for a U.S. Senate
seat as the Republican candidate. His opponent
was Democrat Stephen Douglas, who was up for
reelection. During the campaign, the two men
met several times in what became known as the
Lincoln-Douglas debates. In the debates, Lincoln
was careful not to talk about slavery in the existing
slave states. Instead, he claimed the Democrats were
trying to spread slavery across the nation.

During the second debate, Lincoln questioned
Douglas about popular sovereignty. He wondered
whether that belief went against the *Dred Scott* decision. In other words, how could the people ban
what the Supreme Court allowed? Douglas restated
his belief in popular sovereignty. His response was
remembered as the **Freeport Doctrine**.

> Why do you believe Lincoln would not talk about slavery in the existing slave states?
>
> _____
> _____
> _____

> Why did Lincoln question the Democrats' belief in popular sovereignty?
>
> _____
> _____
> _____

CHALLENGE ACTIVITY

Critical Thinking: Write to Summarize Write a paragraph summarizing
the impact of the Fifth Amendment on the Supreme Court's ruling in
the *Dred Scott* case.

Copyright © by Holt, Rinehart and Winston. All rights reserved.

A Divided Nation

MAIN IDEAS

1. John Brown's raid on Harpers Ferry intensified the disagreement between free states and slave states.

2. The outcome of the election of 1860 divided the United States.

3. The dispute over slavery led the South to secede.

Key Terms and People

John Brown's raid Brown's attack on the Harpers Ferry arsenal, which began October 16, 1859

John C. Breckinridge pro-slavery candidate nominated by southern Democrats for the 1860 presidential election

Constitutional Union Party new political party that concentrated on constitutional principles

John Bell candidate nominated for the 1860 election by the Constitutional Union Party

Confederate States of America the country formed by seceding southern states

Jefferson Davis the Confederacy's first president

John J. Crittenden Tennessee senator who proposed a compromise to try to stop southern secession

Section Summary

RAID ON HARPERS FERRY

John Brown was an abolitionist. He decided to use violence to try to stop slavery. He planned to lead an attack on the arsenal at Harpers Ferry, Virginia.

John Brown's raid began on October 16, 1859. Although he succeeded in taking the arsenal, federal troops overwhelmed him and his small band. They killed some of Brown's followers and captured others, including Brown himself. Brown was charged and found guilty. On December 2, 1859, he was hanged for his crimes.

Many northerners agreed with Brown's anti-slavery beliefs, but they did not agree with his violent methods. Southerners worried that Brown's raid was the start of more attacks on the South.

> **When did John Brown's raid begin?**
> _____
> _____

> **Why do you think John Brown's raid scared southerners?**
> _____
> _____

Copyright © by Holt, Rinehart and Winston. All rights reserved.

Interactive Reader and Study Guide

ELECTION OF 1860

The country was torn as the 1860 presidential election approached. The Democrats proposed two candidates—the North's Stephen Douglas and the South's **John C. Breckinridge**. In addition, the new **Constitutional Union Party** nominated **John Bell**. Abraham Lincoln ran on the Republican ticket.

Lincoln won the election, but he did not carry a southern state in his win. This angered southerners, who worried that they had lost their political power.

> Underline the names of the presidential candidates who ran for election in 1860.

THE SOUTH SECEDES

Southern states responded to Lincoln's election with secession. These states joined together into a new country—the **Confederate States of America**. They elected Mississippian **Jefferson Davis** as their first president. In this country, slavery was legal.

Lincoln argued that southern states could not secede. It seemed that even compromises, like one proposed by Kentucky Senator **John J. Crittenden**, would not mend this tear in the national fabric. President-elect Lincoln declared there could be no compromise where slavery was concerned. He also announced that the federal property in southern lands remained part of the United States.

> Why did southern states secede from the United States of America?
> _____
> _____
> _____
> _____

CHALLENGE ACTIVITY

Critical Thinking: Write to Analyze Write a paragraph explaining why the Democrats ran two candidates in the 1860 presidential election and the affect that had on the South's secession.

Copyright © by Holt, Rinehart and Winston. All rights reserved.

Interactive Reader and Study Guide

The Civil War

CHAPTER SUMMARY

The North and South

Union   **Both**   **Confederacy**

mostly northern anti-slavery states

soldiers endured great hardship

southern pro-slavery states

COMPREHENSION AND CRITICAL THINKING

As you read the section summaries, answer the questions below.

1. **Compare and Contrast** Copy and add to this Venn diagram by adding one phrase or sentence to each area of the diagram.

_____

_____

_____

2. **Make Generalizations** After completing the diagram, what generalization can you make about northern states and the slavery issue?

_____

_____

_____

3. **Make Connections** What events, people, or ideas could you add to the diagram that would help explain the major issues of the war?

_____

_____

_____

_____

Copyright © by Holt, Rinehart and Winston. All rights reserved.

The Civil War

MAIN IDEAS
1. Following the outbreak of war at Fort Sumter, Americans chose sides.
2. The Union and the Confederacy prepared for war.

Key Terms and People

Fort Sumter federal post in Charleston, South Carolina, that surrendered to the Confederacy

border states four slave states—Delaware, Kentucky, Maryland, and Missouri—that bordered the North

Winfield Scott Union general with a two-part strategy for defeating the Confederacy

cotton diplomacy Confederate plan to enlist England's aid in return for continued cotton shipments

Section Summary

AMERICANS CHOOSE SIDES

After being elected in 1861, Abraham Lincoln took office as seven southern states left the Union. He promised he would not end slavery where it existed. However, he also promised to preserve the Union.

Confederate officials already were taking control of federal mints, arsenals, and forts. Fighting finally broke out at **Fort Sumter**, a federal fort in the Confederate state of South Carolina. Federal troops refused to surrender to the Confederacy. Within two days, Fort Sumter fell. Lincoln called for 75,000 militiamen to put down the South's rebellion.

After Lincoln called for troops, all the states had to choose a side. Four more slave states joined the Confederacy. Four **border states**—slave states that bordered the North—decided to stay in the Union. In addition, western Virginia broke off from Confederate Virginia to stay in the Union.

Union General **Winfield Scott** had a two-part strategy to conquer the South. First he would destroy its economy with a naval blockade. Second

How did the South react to Lincoln's election to the presidency?
_____
_____

How did Lincoln respond to the surrender of Fort Sumter?
_____
_____

Copyright © by Holt, Rinehart and Winston. All rights reserved.

Interactive Reader and Study Guide

Section 1, *continued*

he would gain control of the Mississippi River to help divide the South.

The Confederacy had its own plan of attack. Part of that plan involved **cotton diplomacy**—the hope that Britain would support the Confederacy because it needed Confederate cotton. This strategy did not work because Britain had large stores of cotton and got more from India and Egypt.

> Why didn't cotton diplomacy work?
> _____
> _____
> _____

PREPARING FOR WAR

Neither side was prepared for the war to come. However, many citizens—northern and southern— were eager to help. Thousands upon thousands of young men answered the call to arms and volunteered to serve in both armies.

Civilians, too, volunteered to help. They raised money to aid soldiers and their families. They staffed and supplied emergency hospitals. In the Union alone, about 3,000 women served as army nurses.

> In what ways did civilians help the war effort?
> _____
> _____
> _____

Once the thousands of farmers, teachers, laborers, and others joined the armies, they had to be trained to become soldiers. They spent long days drilling and practicing with their guns and bayonets. As a result, many young soldiers were ready to fight.

CHALLENGE ACTIVITY

Critical Thinking: Write to Influence Write an advertisement encouraging people to support the soldiers by coming to a fundraising event.

Copyright © by Holt, Rinehart and Winston. All rights reserved.

The Civil War

Section 2

MAIN IDEAS

1. Union and Confederate forces fought for control of the war in Virginia.
2. The Battle of Antietam gave the North a slight advantage.
3. The Confederacy attempted to break the Union naval blockade.

Key Terms and People

Thomas "Stonewall" Jackson Confederate general who helped fight Union troops at the First Battle of Bull Run

First Battle of Bull Run battle near Manassas Junction, Virginia, in 1861

George B. McClellan general sent by President Lincoln to capture Richmond

Robert E. Lee Confederate general during many important battles of the Civil War

Seven Days' Battles series of battles that forced McClellan to retreat from near Richmond

Second Battle of Bull Run Confederate attack that helped push Union forces out of Virginia

Battle of Antietam battle in Maryland that resulted in Lee's retreat to Virginia

ironclads ships that were heavily armored with iron

Academic Vocabulary

innovation a new idea or way of doing something

Section Summary

WAR IN VIRGINIA

In July 1861, the Union and Confederate armies clashed near Manassas Junction, Virginia, along Bull Run Creek. At first the Union soldiers, under General Irvin McDowell, pushed back the left side of the Confederate line. Then Southern troops, inspired by General **Thomas "Stonewall" Jackson**, fought back. With reinforcements arriving, the Confederate troops drove the Union army back. This conflict, called the **First Battle of Bull Run**, showed that the war would not be an easy victory for the Union.

How did Jackson earn the nickname "Stonewall"?

_____

_____

_____

Copyright © by Holt, Rinehart and Winston. All rights reserved.

After the failed attempt to take Richmond, Lincoln tried again. This time he sent new commander General **George B. McClellan**. In the spring of 1862, McClellan led 100,000 soldiers on a slow march to Richmond.

Then, in June, General **Robert E. Lee** took command of the Confederate forces. On June 26 the two armies met in the **Seven Days' Battles**. These battles pushed McClellan away from Richmond. During the **Second Battle of Bull Run**, Jackson's troops defeated another Union army before it could march directly on Richmond.

> Why did President Lincoln keep sending troops into Virginia?
> _____
> _____
> _____

BATTLE OF ANTIETAM

A copy of Lee's battle strategy left behind led to the next major battle of the Civil War. The Union discovered the Confederates were going to attack Harpers Ferry. McClellan sent his troops to stop them. The **Battle of Antietam** took place on September 17, 1862. It halted Lee's northward march. Despite this success the battle was the bloodiest of the Civil War and of United States history.

> Underline all the Civil War battles identified in this section.

BREAKING THE UNION'S BLOCKADE

Despite the distance it had to control, the Union blockade of Southern ports was very effective. It reduced the number of ships entering southern ports from 6,000 to 800 per year. Even though both sides had the **innovation** of **ironclads**, the Union continued the blockade unbroken.

CHALLENGE ACTIVITY

Critical Thinking: Explain How was a mistake responsible for the Battle of Antietam?

Copyright © by Holt, Rinehart and Winston. All rights reserved.

Interactive Reader and Study Guide

The Civil War

Section 3

> **MAIN IDEAS**
> 1. Union strategy in the West centered on control of the Mississippi River.
> 2. Confederate and Union troops struggled for dominance in the Far West.

Key Terms and People

Ulysses S. Grant Union general whose troops won several important battles on southern soil

Battle of Shiloh battle in which Union troops gained greater control of the Mississippi River valley

David Farragut naval leader who helped the Union take control of New Orleans

Siege of Vicksburg six-week blockade of Vicksburg that starved the city into surrender

Section Summary

UNION STRATEGY IN THE WEST

In February 1862 General **Ulysses S. Grant** led a Union army into Tennessee. He was headed toward the Mississippi River to capture outposts that would separate the eastern Confederacy from its western, food-supplying states. On the way Grant and his forces took both Fort Henry and Fort Donelson.

Near Shiloh Church, Grant halted his troops to wait for more soldiers to arrive. Although Grant was aware of Confederate troops in the area, he was caught by surprise when they attacked on April 6. During the two-day **Battle of Shiloh**, each side lost and gained ground. Union reinforcements arrived and helped push the Confederates into retreating. This win helped the Union control part of the Mississippi River valley.

To control the Mississippi River, the Union had to first deal with New Orleans, the south's largest city and the valuable port near the mouth of the Mississippi River. However, two forts guarded New Orleans from the south.

Union Admiral **David Farragut** solved that problem by racing past the two forts in the darkness

> **Why did the Union consider control of the Mississippi River critical?**
> _____
> _____
> _____

> **How do you know that Fort Henry and Fort Donelson were Confederate forts?**
> _____
> _____
> _____

> **How was New Orleans captured?**
> _____
> _____
> _____

Copyright © by Holt, Rinehart and Winston. All rights reserved.

before dawn on April 24, 1862. Within days New Orleans fell to the Union troops. Farragut continued north, taking more cities, until he reached Vicksburg, Mississippi.

The geography of Vicksburg allowed Confederate General John C. Pemberton to stop any attempt to attack the city. So, instead of trying to attack Vicksburg directly, General Grant cut the city off and shelled it repeatedly. The **Siege of Vicksburg** lasted about six weeks before hunger forced the Confederates to surrender. The Mississippi River was now under Union control.

> **Why was Vicksburg difficult to capture?**
> _____
> _____
> _____

> **Why did the siege of Vicksburg succeed when attacks on Vicksburg had failed?**
> _____
> _____

STRUGGLE FOR THE FAR WEST

Fighting also broke out in the southwest, as the Confederates tried to take control there. Defeats in Arizona and at Glorieta Pass stopped Confederates from taking lands in the West. Confederate-Union conflicts in Missouri also ended with a Confederate defeat, despite aid from the Cherokee. Attacks on Union forts and raids on towns forced the Union commanders to keep valuable troops stationed in the western states and territories.

CHALLENGE ACTIVITY

Critical Thinking: Analyze Write a paragraph analyzing why the Union wanted to control the West.

Copyright © by Holt, Rinehart and Winston. All rights reserved.

MAIN IDEAS

1. The Emancipation Proclamation freed slaves in Confederate states.
2. African Americans participated in the war in a variety of ways.
3. President Lincoln faced opposition to the war.
4. Life was difficult for soldiers and civilians alike.

Key Terms and People

emancipation the freeing of slaves

Emancipation Proclamation announcement freeing Confederate slaves

contrabands escaped slaves

54ᵗʰ Massachusetts Infantry heroic unit of African American soldiers

Copperheads nickname for the Peace Democrats

habeas corpus constitutional protection against unlawful imprisonment

Clara Barton army volunteer whose work became the basis for the American Red Cross

Section Summary

EMANCIPATION PROCLAMATION

President Lincoln realized that one way to weaken the South was to free the slaves. **Emancipation** would free many slaves on which the South's economy relied. After the Battle of Antietam, Lincoln presented the **Emancipation Proclamation**. Despite the impossibility of enforcing it in Confederate-held states, the proclamation still had a distinct effect on the war.

> **What was the purpose of the Emancipation Proclamation?**
> _____
> _____
> _____

AFRICAN AMERICANS PARTICIPATE IN THE WAR

In July 1862 Congress decided to allow African Americans to join the army as laborers. This decision included both free African Americans and **contrabands,** or escaped slaves. Within a year several African American units had formed. The most famous of these was the **54th Massachusetts Infantry,** which helped attack South Carolina's Fort Wagner.

> **How were contrabands different from other African Americans who joined the Union army?**
> _____
> _____

Copyright © by Holt, Rinehart and Winston. All rights reserved.

African American soldiers received less pay than white soldiers. They also faced greater danger because, if captured by Confederates, they could be returned to slavery. In fact Lincoln suggested these soldiers be rewarded by getting the right to vote.

GROWING OPPOSITION

Some mid-westerners did not think the war was necessary. They called themselves Peace Democrats, but their enemies called them **Copperheads**, after the poisonous snake.

Because he saw them as a threat to the war effort, Lincoln had Copperheads put in jail with no evidence and no trial. To do this he ignored their right of **habeas corpus**, the constitutional protection against unlawful imprisonment. Despite this and the northern draft, Lincoln won his second election in 1864.

> **What is habeas corpus?**
> _____
> _____

LIFE FOR SOLDIERS AND CIVILIANS

For the soldier both camplife and combat offered dangers. Poor camp conditions, including lack of medicine and painkillers, led to illness. This alone killed more men than battle did. Those wounded or captured in battle often met the same fate.

Those left behind took over the work of the men who went to war. In addition, many women also provided medical care for the soldiers. For example, volunteer **Clara Barton** formed the organization that would become the American Red Cross.

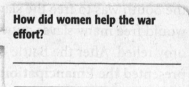

> **How did women help the war effort?**
> _____
> _____

CHALLENGE ACTIVITY

Critical Thinking: Contrast First, imagine you are a lawyer for the Peace Democrats. Write a paragraph explaining why their right of habeas corpus should not be ignored. Then imagine you are a lawyer for the federal government. Write a paragraph defending Lincoln's actions.

Copyright © by Holt, Rinehart and Winston. All rights reserved.

The Civil War

Section 5

MAIN IDEAS

1. The Union tried to divide the Confederate Army at Fredericksburg, but the attempt failed.
2. The Battle of Gettysburg in 1863 was a major turning point in the war.
3. During 1864 Union campaigns in the East and South dealt crippling blows to the Confederacy.
4. Union troops forced the South to surrender in 1865, ending the Civil War.

Key Terms and People

Battle of Gettysburg three-day battle that Confederates lost

George Pickett general who carried out Lee's orders to charge the Union line

Pickett's Charge disastrous attempt by Pickett's troops to storm Cemetery Ridge

Gettysburg Address speech in which Lincoln renewed his commitment to winning the war

Wilderness Campaign series of battles in which Grant tried to take Richmond

William Tecumseh Sherman Union general who cut a path of destruction across Georgia

Total War strategy in which both civilian and military resources are destroyed

Appomattox Courthouse the place where General Lee surrendered to General Grant

Academic Vocabulary

execute to perform, carry out

Section Summary

FREDERICKSBURG AND CHANCELLORSVILLE

In late 1862 Confederate troops under the command of General Robert E. Lee won a battle at Fredericksburg, Virginia. In the spring of 1863, they again defeated Union troops at Chancellorsville.

BATTLE OF GETTYSBURG

Hoping a Confederate win on Union soil would break the Union's spirit, Lee headed into Union territory. The **Battle of Gettysburg**, which started July 1, 1863, was the consequence of Lee's decision.

> **How did the Battle of Gettysburg start?**
>
> _____
>
> _____

Copyright © by Holt, Rinehart and Winston. All rights reserved.

Interactive Reader and Study Guide

The first day, Lee's troops pushed General Meade's soldiers back. The Union troops had to dig in on top of two hills outside the town. On the second day, Confederate troops tried to take the hill called Little Round Top but failed.

On the third day, Lee ordered General **George Pickett** to lead a charge on Cemetery Ridge. **Pickett's Charge** was a disaster. Over half the Confederates were killed, and Lee retreated. Never again would his troops reach northern land.

President Lincoln helped dedicate a new cemetery at Gettysburg. On November 19, 1863, he delivered the **Gettysburg Address**.

> **How long did the Battle of Gettysburg last?**
> _____
> _____

> **Who won the Battle of Gettysburg?**
> _____
> _____

UNION CAMPAIGNS CRIPPLE THE CONFEDERACY

The **Wilderness Campaign** was a series of battles fought in Virginia, around Richmond. Although he lost more men than Lee, Grant also had more reinforcements. As a result of the battles, Grant was winning the war. However, at Petersburg, Lee's defenses did not allow Grant to **execute** his attack and capture Richmond.

To assure his re-election, Lincoln needed a victory. General **William Tecumseh Sherman** provided it by capturing Atlanta, Georgia. This victory helped Lincoln get re-elected in a landslide.

Sherman did not stop at Atlanta. He ordered his troops to cut a path of destruction through Georgia, practicing **total war** all the way to the ocean.

> **Why was the capture of Richmond such an important goal for the Union?**
> _____
> _____
> _____

> **How did General William Sherman help President Lincoln get re-elected?**
> _____
> _____

THE SOUTH SURRENDERS

On April 9, 1865, at **Appomattox Courthouse**, Lee officially surrendered to Grant. The long, bloody war was over, but the question of how the United States could be united again remained.

> **How long did the Civil War last?**
> _____
> _____

CHALLENGE ACTIVITY

Critical Thinking: Make a Time Line Use dates and events in this section to make a time line of the Civil War.

Copyright © by Holt, Rinehart and Winston. All rights reserved.

Reconstruction

CHAPTER SUMMARY

Southern state legislatures begin to pass Black Codes.		Race riots take place in southern towns.	

Even after the Civil War ended slavery, African Americans faced many hardships.

COMPREHENSION AND CRITICAL THINKING

As you read the section summaries, complete the boxes above and answer the questions below.

1. Summarize Describe four things that made post-war life difficult for African Americans.

_____

_____

_____

_____

_____

_____

2. Make Inferences At which level of government did African Americans find the least discrimination during Reconstruction? Explain your answer.

_____

_____

_____

_____

_____

_____

Copyright © by Holt, Rinehart and Winston. All rights reserved.

Interactive Reader and Study Guide

Reconstruction

> **MAIN IDEAS**
> 1. President Lincoln and Congress differed in their views as Reconstruction began.
> 2. The end of the Civil War meant freedom for African Americans in the South.
> 3. President Johnson's plan began the process of Reconstruction.

Key Terms and People

Reconstruction a period of reuniting and rebuilding the South following the end of the Civil War

Ten Percent Plan Lincoln's Reconstruction plan, which required that 10 percent of voters in a state pledge loyalty to the United States before that state could rejoin the Union

Thirteenth Amendment the amendment that made slavery illegal throughout the United States

Freedmen's Bureau an organization established by Congress to provide relief for all the South's poor people

Andrew Johnson vice president who became president upon Lincoln's death

Academic Vocabulary

procedure a series of steps taken to accomplish a task

Section Summary

RECONSTRUCTION BEGINS

As soon as the Civil War ended, Reconstruction began. **Reconstruction** was the process of reuniting the nation and rebuilding the southern states.

President Lincoln proposed that southerners be offered amnesty, or an official pardon. Southerners had to swear an oath of loyalty to the United States and accept the ban on slavery. When 10 percent of the voters in any state took the oath, that state could be accepted back into the Union. This was called the **Ten Percent Plan**.

Some supported the Wade-Davis Bill instead. The **procedure** of the Wade-Davis Bill asked southerners to ban slavery. However, under this bill, most of

> What did the Ten Percent Plan and the Wade-Davis Bill have in common?
> _____
> _____
> _____
> _____

Copyright © by Holt, Rinehart and Winston. All rights reserved.

the people of a state would have to take the pledge before the state could rejoin the Union. Also, only southerners who swore they had never supported the Confederacy could run for office. Lincoln vetoed it.

FREEDOM FOR AFRICAN AMERICANS

In 1865 the **Thirteenth Amendment** to the Constitution officially outlawed slavery in the nation. Former slaves reacted to freedom in many ways. They legalized their marriages, searched for relatives who had been sold, took last names, and moved to new places.

> **What part of the Constitution granted freedom to all slaves?**
> _____
> _____

To help the South's poor and freedpeople Congress created the **Freedmen's Bureau** in 1865. One of its roles was to build more schools. Some freedpeople also established their own schools. Although some southerners violently resisted the idea of educating African Americans, freedpeople of all ages attended classes.

> **Why would southerners oppose the education of African Americans?**
> _____
> _____
> _____
> _____

PRESIDENT JOHNSON'S RECONSTRUCTION PLAN

On April 14, 1865, President Lincoln was shot while attending the theater. He died the next morning. Vice President **Andrew Johnson** became the next president. Johnson's Reconstruction plan included a way to restructure southern state governments. States that followed the steps were to be readmitted to the Union.

Most of the southern states followed Johnson's plan, but Congress refused to accept them back into the Union. Many of the elected representatives of the "new" states had been Confederate leaders. Clearly there were still problems to be solved.

> **Why did Congress refuse to accept the southern states back into the Union?**
> _____
> _____
> _____
> _____

CHALLENGE ACTIVITY

Critical Thinking: Write to Defend You are a citizen from a southern state. Write a letter to Congress defending your right to choose your state's representatives.

Copyright © by Holt, Rinehart and Winston. All rights reserved.

Reconstruction

MAIN IDEAS
1. Black Codes led to opposition to President Johnson's plan for Reconstruction.
2. The Fourteenth Amendment ensured citizenship for African Americans.
3. Radical Republicans in Congress took charge of Reconstruction.
4. The Fifteenth Amendment gave African Americans the right to vote.

Key Terms and People

Black Codes southern laws that greatly limited the freedom of African Americans

Radical Republicans Republicans who wanted more federal control in Reconstruction

Civil Rights Act of 1866 act giving African Americans the same legal rights as whites

Fourteenth Amendment amendment guaranteeing citizens equal protection of laws

Reconstruction Acts laws passed to protect African American rights

impeachment process of bringing charges of wrongdoing against a public official

Fifteenth Amendment amendment guaranteeing suffrage to African American men

Academic Vocabulary

principle basic belief, rule, or law

Section Summary

OPPOSITION TO PRESIDENT JOHNSON

Almost as soon as the southern states created new legislatures, those legislatures went to work passing **Black Codes**. The Black Codes were laws that greatly limited the freedom of African Americans. In fact, the codes created working conditions that resembled slavery for African Americans. Many African Americans organized to protest against the codes.

The Black Codes angered many Republicans who believed the South was returning to its old ways. One group, known as the **Radical Republicans**, wanted the federal government to step in. They wanted more federal control over Reconstruction to make sure southern leaders did not remain loyal to the old Confederate **principles**. One Radical Republican leader was Pennsylvania's Thaddeus

> **Why were the Black Codes passed?**
> _____
> _____
> _____
> _____

Copyright © by Holt, Rinehart and Winston. All rights reserved.

Interactive Reader and Study Guide

Section 2, continued

Stevens. Stevens and others pushed for racial equality. They also branded Johnson's Reconstruction plan a failure.

> Why did Radical Republicans believe President Johnson's Reconstruction plan was a failure?
>
> _____
> _____
> _____
> _____

FOURTEENTH AMENDMENT

In 1866 Congress proposed a bill to give more power to the Freedmen's Bureau. President Johnson vetoed it. He did not believe Congress could pass new laws until the southern states were represented in Congress.

Then Congress proposed the **Civil Rights Act of 1866**. It guaranteed African Americans the same legal rights as whites. Johnson vetoed this, too. Congress overrode the veto. It also proposed the **Fourteenth Amendment** to secure these protections.

> Why did President Johnson veto the Civil Rights Act of 1866?
>
> _____
> _____
> _____
> _____

CONGRESS TAKES CONTROL OF RECONSTRUCTION

After the 1866 elections, Republicans held a two-thirds majority in both the House and Senate. As a result, Congress passed several **Reconstruction Acts**. It also passed a law limiting the president's powers to remove cabinet members without Senate approval. When President Johnson broke that law by firing his secretary of war, Congress reacted by impeaching the president. The **impeachment** fell short by one vote. Johnson remained president, though he had little authority or influence.

FIFTEENTH AMENDMENT

Republicans believed that African Americans would support the Reconstruction plan. To gain their votes, Republicans in Congress proposed the **Fifteenth Amendment**, which guaranteed African American men the right to vote. This amendment went into effect in 1870.

> After the Fifteenth Amendment was ratified, which Americans still could not vote?
>
> _____
> _____

CHALLENGE ACTIVITY

Critical Thinking: Research to Discover In the library or on the Internet, read the Fourteenth and Fifteenth Amendments. Write a sentence paraphrasing each amendment.

Copyright © by Holt, Rinehart and Winston. All rights reserved.

Reconstruction

MAIN IDEAS

1. Reconstruction governments helped reform the South.
2. The Ku Klux Klan was organized as African Americans moved into positions of power.
3. As Reconstruction ended, the rights of African Americans were restricted.
4. Southern business leaders relied on industry to rebuild the South.

Key Terms and People

Hiram Revels first African American senator

Ku Klux Klan secret society that used violence to oppress African Americans

Compromise of 1877 agreement in which Democrats accepted Hayes's election to the presidency in exchange for removing federal troops form the South

poll tax special tax people had to pay before they could vote

segregation forced separation of whites and African Americans in public places

Jim Crow laws laws that enforced segregation

Plessy* v. *Ferguson Supreme Court ruling that upheld segregation

sharecropping system in which farm laborers kept some of the crop

Section Summary

RECONSTRUCTION GOVERNMENTS

After the Civil War, some northern Republicans moved to the South. They were not trusted by southerners who thought the Republicans had come to profit from Reconstruction. African Americans used their new right to vote to elect more than 600 African Americans, including the first black senator, **Hiram Revels**. Together they worked to rebuild the war-damaged South.

> Why were African Americans elected if overall they were in the minority?
> _____
> _____
> _____
> _____

KU KLUX KLAN

Many southerners opposed Reconstruction. In 1866 a group of them created the secret and violent **Ku Klux Klan**. Its targets were African Americans, Republicans, and public officials. The Klan spread throughout the South until the federal government

> Circle the groups of Americans that were targeted by the Ku Klux Klan.

Copyright © by Holt, Rinehart and Winston. All rights reserved.

stepped in and passed laws that made Klan activities
illegal. Violence, however, continued.

RECONSTRUCTION ENDS

The General Amnesty Act of 1872 allowed most
former Confederates to serve in public office. Soon
many Democratic ex-Confederates were elected.
Republicans also lost power as a consequence of
Grant's problem-plagued presidency and the Panic
of 1873. In 1876 the Hayes-Tilden presidential race
was so close it took the **Compromise of 1877** to
make sure Democats would accept Hayes's election.

> **Why did southern Republicans lose power during the 1870s?**
>
> _____
> _____
> _____
> _____

Southern Democrats, called Redeemers, worked
to limit African American rights. The methods they
used included **poll taxes**, legal **segregation**, and **Jim
Crow laws**. They even got help from the Supreme
Court, which ruled in *Plessy* v. *Ferguson* that segregation was legal.

Africans Americans found their rights restricted
in other ways, too. Most African Americans could
not afford to buy land, so many began **sharecropping**, or sharing the crop with landowners. Often
only the landowner profited, while sharecroppers
lived in debt.

REBUILDING SOUTHERN INDUSTRY

The South's economy depended on cotton profits, which went up and down. In the "New South"
movement, southern leaders turned to industry to
strengthen the economy. Mills and factories were
built. The new industries thrived and helped the
southern economy grow stronger.

> **How was the economy of the "Old South" different from the economy of the "New South"?**
>
> _____
> _____
> _____

CHALLENGE ACTIVITY

Critical Thinking: Write to Put in Sequence Write a paragraph explaining how the General Amnesty Act eventually led to the Compromise of
1877.

Copyright © by Holt, Rinehart and Winston. All rights reserved.

Americans Move West

CHAPTER SUMMARY

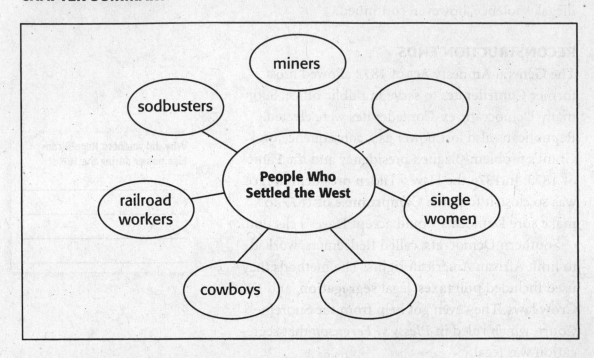

miners

sodbusters

People Who Settled the West

single women

railroad workers

cowboys

COMPREHENSION AND CRITICAL THINKING

As you read the section summaries, complete the ovals above and answer the questions below.

1. Identify Look at the graphic organizer above. What other groups came to settle the West?

_____

_____

_____

2. Make Judgments Should the settlement web above have more then seven ovals? Why or why not?

_____

_____

_____

_____

_____

_____

Copyright © by Holt, Rinehart and Winston. All rights reserved.

Americans Move West

Section 1

MAIN IDEAS
1. A mining boom brought growth to the West.
2. The demand for cattle created a short-lived Cattle Kingdom on the Great Plains.
3. East and West were connected by the transcontinental railroad.

Key Terms and People

frontier an area that is undeveloped

Comstock Lode name given to 1859 gold and silver discovery in western Nevada

boomtowns towns that serviced new mines and emptied when the mines closed

Cattle Kingdom the name given to the Great Plains during the years when they supported great herds of cattle

cattle drive movement of cattle herds to market or new grazing lands

Chisholm Trail a popular route for cattle drives from San Antonio to Abilene, Kansas

Pony Express mail delivery system in which messengers transported mail on horseback across the country

transcontinental railroad railroad across United States, connecting East and West

Academic Vocabulary

establish to set up or create

Section Summary

MINING BOOM BRINGS GROWTH

After the Civil War, many Americans moved west. Most passed through the dry Great Plains and went on to California. By 1850 the **frontier**, or undeveloped region, had reached the Pacific Ocean.

Eventually, new farming techniques, fewer attacks by Native Americans, and railroads brought people to the Great Plains. Newcomers relied on railroads to get their goods to market.

In 1859 miners found gold and silver in western Nevada. News of the **Comstock Lode** (named after miner Henry Comstock) brought thousands to Nevada. Most miners eventually were bought out

> Why did pioneers finally decide to settle in the Great Plains?
>
> _____
> _____
> _____
> _____

Copyright © by Holt, Rinehart and Winston. All rights reserved.

by big business, which could afford the equipment needed to remove precious metals from quartz. Mining jobs were dangerous and low paying. Many immigrants came to work in the mines. As mines opened, **boomtowns** were **established**. When the mines closed down, most boomtowns did, too.

> How did the discovery of precious metals effect Nevada's population?
> _____
> _____

THE CATTLE KINGDOM

Demand for beef in the East led to a booming cattle industry in Texas. Soon the cattle industry spread onto the Great Plains, creating a huge **Cattle Kingdom** with giant herds grazing the open range.

> Circle the sentence that helps you to infer that cattle need large parcels of land for grazing.

Cowboys cared for the cattle. They were responsible for the long **cattle drives** that got the cattle to Abilene, Kansas. There, the new railroad could ship the cattle to markets far away. The **Chisholm Trail** was one of the routes used for this journey.

THE TRANSCONTINENTAL RAILROAD

In 1860 the **Pony Express** improved communication between the East and the West. But it was replaced in 1861 by the telegraph, which could send messages much faster.

By 1862 Congress started passing laws that supported the building of a **transcontinental railroad**. By the end of 1863, the work had begun. One railroad line was building from the East and one from the West. In 1869 the two lines met at Promontory, Utah. Soon, railroads crisscrossed the country.

> Based on what you have read, how would you define the word *transcontinental*?
> _____
> _____

Railroads provided better transportation for people and goods all over America. By 1890 railroads were one of the nation's biggest industries.

CHALLENGE ACTIVITY

Critical Thinking: Evaluate Research the Pony Express to find out why it operated for only 18 months. Write an essay giving your opinion about whether the Pony Express was a success.

Copyright © by Holt, Rinehart and Winston. All rights reserved.

Americans Move West

Section 2

MAIN IDEAS

1. As settlers moved to the Great Plains, they encountered the Plains Indians.
2. The U.S. Army and Native Americans fought in the northern plains, the Southwest, and the Far West.
3. Despite efforts to reform U.S. policy toward Native Americans, conflict continued.

Key Terms and People

Treaty of Fort Laramie first major agreement signed with northern Plains nations

reservations areas of federal land set aside for Native Americans

Crazy Horse Sioux leader who violently protested reservations

Treaty of Medicine Lodge southern Plains Indians agreed to live on reservations

buffalo soldiers nickname given by Indians to African American cavalry

George Armstrong Custer army commander who lost to the Sioux at Little Bighorn

Sitting Bull Sioux leader who defeated Custer at Little Bighorn

Battle of the Little Bighorn last great victory for Sioux, in which they defeated Custer

Massacre at Wounded Knee battle in which U.S. troops killed about 150 Sioux

Long Walk a 300-mile forced march of Navajo captives to a New Mexico reservation

Geronimo Apache leader who continued to fight against the U.S. Army until 1886

Ghost Dance religious movement predicting a coming paradise for Native Americans

Sarah Winnemucca Paiute against the government's treatment of Native Americans

Dawes General Allotment Act act that took back almost 70 percent of reservation land

Section Summary

SETTLERS ENCOUNTER THE PLAINS INDIANS

The **Treaty of Fort Laramie** was one of the first treaties the government signed to keep peace with the Plains Indians. Other treaties created **reservations** for Indians. Many Indians refused to move to the reservations. In 1864 U.S. soldiers killed about 200 Cheyenne in the Sand Creek Massacre. In 1866 **Crazy Horse** and his Sioux warriors killed about 81 soldiers. By the 1867 **Treaty of Medicine Lodge**, most southern Plains Indians agreed to go to reservations.

> What was the purpose of early treaties between the U.S. government and Native Americans?
>
> _____
>
> _____
>
> _____

> Why do you think that many Native Americans fought the move to reservations?
>
> _____
>
> _____
>
> _____

Copyright © by Holt, Rinehart and Winston. All rights reserved.

FIGHTING ON THE PLAINS

Native Americans of the northern Plains, Southwest, and Far West continued to resist reservations. The U.S. government sent **buffalo soldiers** and other troops to force Indians to leave.

In 1874 gold was discovered in the Black Hills of the Dakotas. The government wanted the Sioux to sell their reservation. **Sitting Bull** and other Sioux refused. In response, Lieutenant Colonel **George Armstrong Custer** ordered his soldiers to attack the Sioux. The Sioux won what became known as the **Battle of Little Bighorn**. In the last great battle of the Plains Indians, 150 Sioux were killed in the **Massacre at Wounded Knee.**

Other Native Americans also fought being forced onto reservations. The Navajo of the Southwest tried to resist, but facing starvation, began to surrender. They were led on a forced march to a reservation that became known as the **Long Walk**. Many died along the way. In 1886 Apache leader **Geronimo** and his warrior band surrendered, which ended Apache armed resistance.

> **Why did the government want the Sioux to sell their reservation?**
> _____
> _____

CONFLICT CONTINUES

In the 1870s the **Ghost Dance** was a religious movement started by a Paiute leader named Wovoka. It predicted paradise for Indians. But officials feared this movement would lead to rebellion. Another Paiute, **Sarah Winnemucca**, lectured on problems with the reservation system. In 1887 Congress passed the **Dawes General Allotment Act**, which gave U.S. citizenship to Native Americans. However, it took back two thirds of the land originally set aside for them.

> **Why would officials worry about the spread of the Ghost Dance beliefs?**
> _____
> _____

CHALLENGE ACTIVITY

Critical Thinking: Write to Evaluate In a paragraph describe how you think the public reacted to Custer's defeat.

Copyright © by Holt, Rinehart and Winston. All rights reserved.

Interactive Reader and Study Guide

Americans Move West

MAIN IDEAS

1. Many Americans started new lives on the Great Plains.
2. Economic challenges led to the creation of farmers' political groups.
3. By the 1890s, the western frontier had come to an end.

Key Terms and People

Homestead Act an 1862 act that gave government-owned land to farmers

Morrill Act an 1862 act that gave government-owned land to the states, with the understanding that the states would sell the land to finance colleges

Exodusters African Americans who left the South for Kansas in 1879

sodbusters nickname given Great Plains farmers because of the toughness of the soil

dry farming farming using hardy crops that need less water than others

Annie Bidwell a Great Plains pioneer-reformer

deflation a decrease in the money supply and overall lower prices

National Grange a social and educational organization for farmers

William Jennings Bryan Democratic candidate for president in the 1888 election

Populist Party new national party formed by the country's farmers

Academic Vocabulary

facilitate to make easier

Section Summary

NEW LIVES ON THE PLAINS

In 1862 two acts helped open the West to settlers. The **Homestead Act** gave government-owned land to small farmers. The **Morrill Act** gave government land to the states. The states would then sell that land and use the money to build colleges.

These acts attracted many groups to the Great Plains. This included single women, who could get land through the Homestead Act. It also included up to 40,000 African Americans. Some called them **Exodusters** because of their exodus from the South. **Sodbusters** earned their nickname because breaking up the sod of the Great plains was hard work.

> Circle the two congressional acts in 1862 that helped settle the West.

> How did sodbusters get their nickname?
>
> _____
>
> _____

Copyright © by Holt, Rinehart and Winston. All rights reserved.

Dry farming helped the sodbusters succeed. Cyrus McCormick also **facilitated** farming with his new mechanical farming equipment.

Some pioneer women, such as author Laura Ingalls Wilder and suffragist **Annie Bidwell**, became famous. Most though lived a lonely life on the remote farms of the plains. Early farmers also had to build their own communities.

FARMERS' POLITICAL GROUPS

Modern machines made farming more productive. This productivity, however, led to overproduction, which in turn led to lower crop prices. To make matters worse, at this time the U.S. economy was affected by **deflation**, in which the money supply decreased and prices dropped. So although farmers farmed more, they made less money for their crops. Many lost their farms during this time.

To help each other, farmers formed the **National Grange** (*grange* is an old word for "granary"). The Grange worked to better farmers' lives. It worked to get the railroads regulated. It also backed political candidates such as **William Jennings Bryan**.

In 1892 political organizations called Farmers' Alliances formed a new pro-farmer political party. They called it the **Populist Party**. In the 1896 presidential elections, it supported Democrat Bryan. Bryan lost and the Populist Party dissolved.

> **Why could banding together help farmers?**
> _____
> _____
> _____

> **Why do you think the Populist Party dissolved after Bryan lost the presidential election?**
> _____
> _____
> _____

END OF THE FRONTIER

In 1889, the government opened Oklahoma to homesteaders. These pioneers quickly claimed more than 11 million acres of land. The frontier existed no more.

> **What ended America's frontier?**
> _____
> _____

CHALLENGE ACTIVITY

Critical Thinking: Write to Connect Explain why overproduction on farms could lead to lower prices for crops.

Copyright © by Holt, Rinehart and Winston. All rights reserved.

Interactive Reader and Study Guide

The Industrial Age

CHAPTER SUMMARY

CAUSE		EFFECT
The Bessemer Process makes steel quicker and cheaper to produce.	⟶	Demand for steel rises
	⟶	Transportation improves
Carnegie, Rockefeller, and other business giants form trusts to monopolize industries.	⟶	
Workers work long hours for very little money.	⟶	Workers form labor unions

COMPREHENSION AND CRITICAL THINKING

As you read the section summaries, complete the table above and answer the questions below.

1. Cause and Effect What innovations changed American life in the 1800s?

_____

_____

_____

_____

_____

2. Make Inferences Did the national government approve or disapprove of trusts? How can you tell?

_____

_____

_____

_____

_____

_____

_____

Copyright © by Holt, Rinehart and Winston. All rights reserved.

Interactive Reader and Study Guide

Name _____ Class _____ Date _____

The Industrial Age

MAIN IDEAS

1. Breakthroughs in steel processing led to a boom in railroad construction.
2. Advances in the use of oil and electricity improved communications and transportation.
3. A rush of inventions changed Americans' lives.

Key Terms and People

Second Industrial Revolution a period of rapid growth in U.S. manufacturing in the late 1800s

Bessemer process Henry Bessemer's invention that made steel production faster and cheaper

Thomas Edison inventor who created the electric lightbulb

patent an exclusive right to make or sell an invention

Alexander Graham Bell inventor of the telephone

Henry Ford inventor of the first affordable car and the moving assembly line

Wilbur and Orville Wright brothers who made the first piloted flight in a gas-powered airplane

Academic Vocabulary

implement to put in place

Section Summary

BREAKTHROUGHS IN STEEL PROCESSING

America's **Second Industrial Revolution** started in the late 1800s. The new **Bessemer process** reduced the amount of time it took to make steel. The price of steel dropped because of this innovation. This made the steel industry an important part of the revolution.

Cheaper, more available steel led to more railroad building. Other changes made train travel safer and smoother for passengers. Trains helped strengthen the economy by moving people and goods to their destinations quickly and inexpensively.

> What effect did inexpensive, readily available steel have on the railroad industry?
> _____
> _____
> _____
> _____

Copyright © by Holt, Rinehart and Winston. All rights reserved.

Interactive Reader and Study Guide

USE OF OIL AND ELECTRICITY

In the 1850s scientists figured out how to turn crude oil into kerosene. Kerosene was used for both heat and light. As a result, the demand for oil exploded. In 1859 Edwin L. Drake's Titusville, Pennsylvania, oil well started producing 20 barrels of oil a day. Oil quickly became big business in Pennsylvania. Oil was also important in Ohio and West Virginia.

In addition to oil, electricity became a source of light and power. **Thomas Edison** was an inventor interested in uses of electricity. In 1879 Edison and his assistant created the electric lightbulb. To create a market for his product, Edison built a power plant to supply industries with electricity. George Westinghouse developed a power plant that could send electricity over long distances. Thanks to Edison and Westinghouse the use of electricity in homes and business boomed.

> What made the demand for oil rise in the 1850s?
> _____
> _____
> _____

> How did Edison and Westinghouse help spread the use of electricity?
> _____
> _____
> _____

RUSH OF INVENTIONS

Technology also changed the way people communicated. First, telegraphs made long-distance communication possible. Then in 1876 **Alexander Graham Bell** was given a **patent** for the telephone. By 1900 almost 1.5 million telephones were in operation.

Changes in transportation also occurred. The invention of the gasoline-powered engine made automobiles possible. **Henry Ford** began producing the first affordable automobile in 1908. He also **implemented** the moving assembly line in manufacturing. The gas-powered engine allowed **Wilbur and Orville Wright** to invent the airplane.

> What made the technological advances of the late nineteenth century possible?
> _____
> _____
> _____

CHALLENGE ACTIVITY

Critical Thinking: Write to Make Judgments Review all of the inventions about which you just read. In your opinion, which was the most life-changing? Why?

Copyright © by Holt, Rinehart and Winston. All rights reserved.

The Industrial Age

> **MAIN IDEAS**
> 1. The rise of corporations and powerful business leaders led to the dominance of big businesses in the United States.
> 2. People and the government began to question the methods of big business.

Key Terms and People

corporations businesses owned by stockholders

Andrew Carnegie business leader who concentrated his efforts on steel production

vertical integration owning the businesses involved in each step of manufacturing

John D. Rockefeller business leader who concentrated on oil refining

horizontal integration owning all of the businesses in a certain field

trust a legal arrangement grouping together a number of companies under a single board of directors

Leland Stanford business leader of mining equipment and railroads

social Darwinism belief that Charles Darwin's theory of natural selection and "survival of the fittest" holds true for humans

monopoly total ownership of a product or service

Sherman Antitrust Act law that made it illegal to monopolize a business

Academic Vocabulary

acquired to get

Section Summary

DOMINANCE OF BIG BUSINESS

In the late 1800s entrepreneurs began to form **corporations**. A corporation is owned by people who buy shares of stock in that corporation. Stockholders share the corporation's profits. But if the corporation fails, stockholders lose the money that they invested. Entrepreneurs could spread the risk of loss across all the stockholders.

One successful entrepreneur of the late 1800s was **Andrew Carnegie**. He made money in several industries, but he focused on steel. Carnegie

> Why did entrepreneurs form corporations in the late 1800s?
>
> _____
> _____
> _____

Copyright © by Holt, Rinehart and Winston. All rights reserved.

Interactive Reader and Study Guide

acquired all of the businesses involved in making steel. This process is called **vertical integration**.

John D. Rockefeller made his fortune in oil. Like Carnegie, he used vertical integration. He also used **horizontal integration**, buying out most of his competitors. He grouped his companies into a **trust** in an effort to control oil production and prices.

Leland Stanford was another successful business leader of the time. He made money selling mining equipment to miners. He also helped found the California Central Pacific railroad.

> How did entrepreneurs benefit from vertical integration and horizontal integration?
> _____
> _____
> _____

QUESTIONING THE METHODS OF BIG BUSINESS

In the late 1800s many business leaders believed in **social Darwinism**. Charles Darwin proposed that in nature, the law was "survival of the fittest." Social Darwinists believed the same was true of humans—those who got rich were the fittest.

> What is social Darwinism?
> _____
> _____
> _____

Other wealthy business leaders claimed that the rich had a duty to help the poor. As a result, some leaders gave millions of dollars to charities.

Big business caused problems for small businesses. A big business would lower its prices until small businesses, unable to offer the same low prices, went bankrupt. Consumers then had to pay higher prices because there was no longer any competition.

> Why did some people think trusts were bad for society?
> _____
> _____
> _____

Americans demanded that Congress pass laws to control **monopolies** and trusts. Congress finally passed the **Sherman Antitrust Act**. However the act was weak and did little to reduce the power of corporations.

CHALLENGE ACTIVITY

Critical Thinking: Evaluate You are an adviser to the president. Voters are complaining about big discount stores putting small, family-owned stores out of business by lowering prices. Make a list of advantages and disadvantages of large stores. Write a summary of your list and advise the president what to do.

Copyright © by Holt, Rinehart and Winston. All rights reserved.

The Industrial Age

MAIN IDEAS

1. The desire to maximize profits and become more efficient led to poor working conditions.

2. Workers began to organize and demand improvements in working conditions and pay.

3. Labor strikes often turned violent and failed to accomplish their goals.

Key Terms and People

Frederick W. Taylor author of *The Principles of Scientific Management*

Knights of Labor large labor union that included both skilled and unskilled workers

Terence V. Powderly Knights of Labor leader who made it the first national labor union in the United States

Samuel Gompers leader of the American Federation of Labor

American Federation of Labor group that organized individual national unions of skilled workers

collective bargaining workers acting together for better wages or working conditions

Mary Harris Jones union supporter who organized strikes and educated workers

Haymarket Riot a union protest in Chicago where strikers fought with police

Homestead strike violent 1892 strike of Carnegie steelworkers ended by state militia

Pullman strike strike of Pullman railroad workers that ended in 1894 when federal troops were sent to stop it

Section Summary

MAXIMIZING PROFITS AND EFFICIENCY

During the Second Industrial Revolution, machines did more and more work. The unskilled workers who ran the machines could not complain about conditions, for they knew they could be replaced.

In the early 1880s **Frederick W. Taylor** wrote a book that took a scientific look at how businesses could increase profits. One way was to ignore workers and their needs. As a result, conditions for workers got worse.

> What impact did Frederick Taylor's book have on America's workers?
>
> _____
>
> _____
>
> _____

Copyright © by Holt, Rinehart and Winston. All rights reserved.

WORKERS ORGANIZE

Workers began to form labor unions. The **Knights of Labor** started out as a secret organization. However by the end of the 1870s, under the leadership of **Terence V. Powderly**, the Knights became a national labor union. The Knights included both skilled and unskilled members.

The **American Federation of Labor**, under the leadership of **Samuel Gompers**, was different from the Knights of Labor. It organized national unions, and its members were all skilled workers.

Workers hoped that if they acted together—that is, if they used **collective bargaining**—they might actually be able to improve pay and working conditions.

Many women participated in unions. **Mary Harris Jones**, for example, helped organize strikes and educate workers.

> **Which union would have more power—a union of unskilled workers or a union of skilled workers?**
> _____
> _____
> _____

> **How did workers benefit from collective bargaining?**
> _____
> _____
> _____

LABOR STRIKES

In 1886 thousands of Chicago union members went on strike. After police killed two strikers, workers met at Haymarket Square to protest the killings. Someone threw a bomb, and officers fired into the crowd. The **Haymarket Riot** ended with more than 100 people killed or wounded.

On June 29, 1892, at a Carnegie steel plant in Homestead, Pennsylvania, the **Homestead strike** began. Workers protested the introduction of new machinery and the loss of jobs. It ended in violence and death, and the union was defeated. Two years later, the **Pullman strike** over layoffs and pay cuts also ended in bloodshed. President Grover Cleveland sent federal troops to break the strike.

> **Why do you think labor strikes often ended in violence?**
> _____
> _____
> _____

CHALLENGE ACTIVITY

Critical Thinking: Write to Explain Explain why workers sometimes use strikes as a strategy.

Copyright © by Holt, Rinehart and Winston. All rights reserved.

Immigrants and Urban Life

CHAPTER SUMMARY

Old immigrants	*settled in*	small towns and rural areas.
New immigrants	*settled in*	
	led to	unsafe and unsanitary living conditions.
Reformers	*worked to*	

COMPREHENSION AND CRITICAL THINKING

As you read the section summaries, fill in the blanks in the table above and answer the questions below.

1. Identify Cause and Effect What effect did the arrival of millions of immigrants have on the United States?

_____

_____

2. Evaluate Do you think that the unsanitary conditions in large cities could have been avoided? Why or why not?

_____

_____

_____

_____

3. Identify Cause and Effect Many reformers used newspapers and other publications to show tenement living conditions. How do you think this helped improve people's lives?

_____

_____

_____

Copyright © by Holt, Rinehart and Winston. All rights reserved.

Immigrants and Urban Life

> **MAIN IDEAS**
> 1. U.S. immigration patterns changed during the late 1800s as new immigrants arrived from Europe, Asia, and Mexico.
> 2. Immigrants worked hard to adjust to life in the United States.
> 3. Some Americans opposed immigration and worked to restrict it.

Key Terms and People

old immigrants people who arrived from northern Europe in the mid-1800s

new immigrants people who arrived from southern and eastern Europe in the late 1800s

steerage an area below a ship's deck where immigrants often traveled

benevolent societies organizations that offered help to immigrant families

tenements poorly built, overcrowded apartment buildings

sweatshops workplaces in small shops with poor working conditions and low pay

Chinese Exclusion Act law in 1880 banning immigration by Chinese people for ten years

Academic Vocabulary

advocate to plead in favor of

Section Summary

CHANGING PATTERNS OF IMMIGRATION

During the mid-1800s, millions of immigrants came to the United States from northern Europe. Many of these **old immigrants** were skilled workers or farmers. Most were Protestants. Later, many **new immigrants** came from different places, including southern and eastern Europe. These immigrants came from many different cultures and religions.

Immigrants usually faced a difficult journey by ship to America, often travelling in **steerage**. Then they faced the challenge of actually getting into the United States. Many European immigrants entered at Ellis Island in New York Harbor. On the West Coast, many Chinese immigrants entered the United States through Angel Island near

> Where did most of the new immigrants come from?
>
> _____
>
> _____

> Underline two major points of entry for immigrants to the United States in the late 1800s.

Copyright © by Holt, Rinehart and Winston. All rights reserved.

Section 1, *continued*

San Francisco. In the Southwest, Mexican immigrants came to the United States through El Paso, Texas.

ADJUSTING TO A NEW LIFE

After entering the United States, immigrants had to adjust to life in a different country. They had to learn new customs and a new language. Many of them moved into neighborhoods with other people from the same country. Immigrant neighborhoods often had schools, clubs, newspapers, shops, and banks. These helped people start their new lives. **Benevolent societies** helped families in case of sickness, unemployment, or death.

Many new immigrants came from rural areas. They lacked the skills to work in modern manufacturing or industrial work. As a result, many of them had to take low-paying unskilled manufacturing jobs in large factories and **sweatshops.** Their low-paying jobs often forced them to live in **tenements.**

> Why did many immigrants have to take low paying jobs in sweatshops?
>
> _____
>
> _____

OPPOSITION TO IMMIGRATION

Some Americans welcomed new immigrants. Others feared that immigrants would take away jobs from native-born Americans. Nativists believed that too many immigrants were being allowed into the country. This led to a growth in anti-immigrant feelings in the late 1800s.

Some people **advocated** laws to limit immigration. Congress passed the **Chinese Exclusion Act,** which banned immigration from China for ten years. A later law restricted convicts, people who had certain diseases, and those likely to need public assistance. Immigrants continued to arrive in large numbers and worked to achieve their dreams.

> What was the purpose of the Chinese Exclusion Act?
>
> _____
>
> _____

CHALLENGE ACTIVITY

Critical Thinking: Write to Influence Write a letter to the editor of a newspaper in the late 1880s. Explain why you think there should or should not be limits on the number of immigrants to the United States.

Copyright © by Holt, Rinehart and Winston. All rights reserved.

Interactive Reader and Study Guide

Immigrants and Urban Life

> **MAIN IDEAS**
> 1. Both immigrants and native-born Americans moved to growing urban areas in record numbers in the late 1800s and early 1900s.
> 2. New technology and ideas helped cities change and adapt to rapid population growth.

Key Terms and People

mass transit public transportation designed to move a large number of people

suburbs residential neighborhoods outside of downtown areas

mass culture leisure and cultural activities shared by many people

Joseph Pulitzer publisher of *New York World* newspaper

William Randolph Hearst publisher of *New York Journal* newspaper

department stores large retail stores that sell many different types of goods

Frederick Law Olmsted landscape architect who designed Central Park in New York City

Academic Vocabulary

factor cause

Section Summary

GROWTH OF URBAN AREAS

During the late 1800s many native-born Americans and immigrants moved to cities. By 1900, about 40 percent of Americans lived in cities. The people moving into large cities included new immigrants and rural residents looking for work. Farm equipment replaced workers in rural areas. African Americans from the rural South moved to northern cities. They wanted to escape discrimination and find better opportunities.

Between 1850 and 1900, Chicago grew from 30,000 people to 1.7 million. Many of the new residents were immigrants from southern and eastern Europe. One **factor** in the growth of Chicago was its location on new railroad lines. These rail lines

> **Why did many African Americans move from southern farm areas to northern cities?**
> _____
> _____

Copyright © by Holt, Rinehart and Winston. All rights reserved.

Interactive Reader and Study Guide

placed Chicago in the center of the trade in lumber, grain, and meat.

CHANGING CITIES

New technology helped cities grow quickly and changed the look of American cities. One way to find space for people to live and work was to build taller buildings. The steel industry grew in the late 1800s. Steel beams became inexpensive enough to use in frames of tall buildings. The invention of the safety elevator made skyscrapers practical.

Skyscrapers made it possible for more people to work and live in the cities. **Mass transit** developed, allowing people to travel in large numbers. Mass transit let many middle-class residents move to **suburbs.**

> How did the development of mass transit lead to growth of suburbs?
> _____
> _____

As the publishing industry grew, **mass culture** developed in the United States. Big cities often had many competing newspapers. The *New York World,* published by **Joseph Pulitzer** and the *New York Journal,* published by **William Randolph Hearst**, fought for readership in New York City. Huge **department stores** changed the way people shopped for goods in cities.

> List some examples of things that are part of today's mass culture.
> _____
> _____
> _____

The demand for public entertainment led to large fairs and the creation of amusement parks. People also needed open public space in large cities. **Frederick Law Olmsted** became famous for designing Central Park in New York City, as well as many state and national parks.

> Underline the sentence that explains why large fairs and amusement parks were developed.

CHALLENGE ACTIVITY

Critical Thinking: Analyze During the second half of the nineteenth century, new inventions made farming much more efficient. How did these inventions promote the growth of cities?

Copyright © by Holt, Rinehart and Winston. All rights reserved.

MAIN IDEAS
1. Crowded urban areas faced a variety of social problems.
2. People worked to improve the quality of life in U.S. cities.

Key Terms and People

Jacob Riis journalist and photographer who exposed the horrible conditions in New York City tenements

settlement houses neighborhood centers in poor areas that offered education, recreation, and social activities

Jane Addams founder of Hull House

Hull House Chicago's most famous settlement house

Florence Kelley Chicago reformer who worked to pass child labor laws

Section Summary

URBAN PROBLEMS

Even with new technology, many cities were not ready for the population growth of the late 1800s. There was a shortage of affordable housing which led to overcrowding and poor living conditions. Many poor families were squeezed into tiny tenement apartments. **Jacob Riis** became famous for his articles and photographs that exposed the horrible conditions in the tenements.

The overcrowding caused sanitation problems and unsafe living conditions. Garbage collection systems were not efficient, so garbage piled up in the cities. Indoor plumbing was scarce, and water supplies became polluted. Fires could spread rapidly, but fire escapes were often blocked.

These conditions caused the spread of disease-causing bacteria. There were outbreaks of diseases such as typhoid, cholera, influenza, and tuberculosis. As a result, about half of the babies born died before the age of five. The overcrowded living conditions and the manufacturing industries also caused serious air pollution problems.

> What did Jacob Riis do to help change conditions in tenement apartments?
> _____
> _____

> Underline the sentences that describe the sanitation problems caused by crowded conditions in cities.

Copyright © by Holt, Rinehart and Winston. All rights reserved.

City governnments worked to reduce these problems by hiring firefighters and police officers. New sewage and drinking water purification systems helped reduce the sanitation problem.

> **What did cities do to relieve the health and safety problems caused by crowding?**
>
> _____
>
> _____

IMPROVING CITY LIFE

Reformers worked to improve living conditions in the tenements. In 1901, new laws in New York State required better ventilation and running water in new buildings. Other states followed New York's lead.

Private organizations also helped the urban poor. Some people developed **settlement houses** in neighborhoods to provide education, recreation, and social activities. These settlement houses had professionals and volunteers on staff, including educated women from wealthy families. Some of these houses are still active today.

> **Were the settlement houses founded by public or private organizations?**
>
> _____
>
> _____

Jane Addams founded **Hull House** in Chicago, the most famous settlement house. Addams and Ellen Gates Starr moved into a rundown building and turned it into Hull House. The staff served the needs of immigrant families. It provided English classes, day care, cooking and sewing classes, and other services.

The Hull House staff also worked for reforms to improve conditions for poor families. **Florence Kelley** visited sweatshops and wrote about the problems she saw there. She helped convince lawmakers in Illinois to pass a law limiting work hours for women and preventing child labor. She later became the chief factory inspector for the state and helped enforce the law.

CHALLENGE ACTIVITY

Critical Thinking: Analyze As the cities grew rapidly, crowded conditions created many problems. Why didn't the people just move away from the cities to find better conditions?

Copyright © by Holt, Rinehart and Winston. All rights reserved.

The Progressive Spirit of Reform

CHAPTER SUMMARY

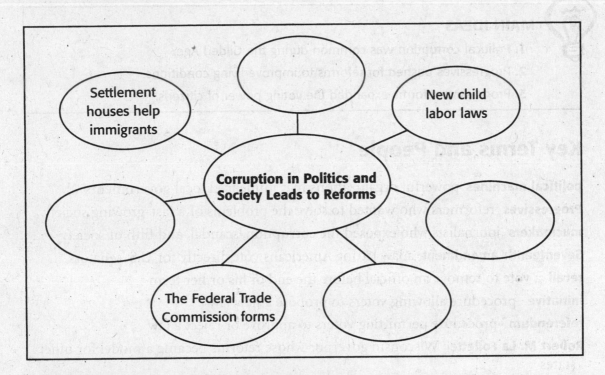

COMPREHENSION AND CRITICAL THINKING

As you read the section summaries, fill in the blanks in the graphic
organizer above and answer the questions below.

1. **Identify** Identify four additional reform efforts made in the later 1800s and early
   1900s. Add them to the web above.

2. **Make Judgments** Of the reforms you have identified, which was the most important? Write a sentence defending your opinion.

   _____

   _____

   _____

   _____

3. **Make Connections** Where did the pressure to reform government come from?
   How did the progressive presidents respond to this pressure?

   _____

   _____

   _____

   _____

Copyright © by Holt, Rinehart and Winston. All rights reserved.

The Progressive Spirit of Reform

MAIN IDEAS
1. Political corruption was common during the Gilded Age.
2. Progressives pushed for reforms to improve living conditions.
3. Progressive reforms expanded the voting power of citizens.

Key Terms and People

political machines powerful organizations that influenced local governments

Progressives reformers who wanted to solve the problems of a fast-growing society

muckrakers journalists who exposed the corruption, scandal, and filth of society

Seventeenth Amendment a law letting Americans vote directly for U.S. senators

recall a vote to remove an official before the end of his or her term

initiative procedure allowing voters to propose a new law

referendum procedure permitting voters to approve or reject a law

Robert M. La Follette Wisconsin governor whose reforms became a model for other states

Academic Vocabulary

motive a reason for doing something

Section Summary

POLITICAL CORRUPTION

During the Gilded Age, governments were riddled with corruption. **Political machines** controlled most local politics. Illegal activities included buying votes, bribing vote counters, and stuffing ballot boxes with extra votes. Both of President Ulysses S. Grant's terms were very corrupt. Some members of Congress were involved in a railroad scandal, causing widespread public distrust.

> What illegal activities did political machines use to change election results?
> _____
> _____

Many of the jobs with the civil service were given to political supporters rather than to qualified candidates. Presidents Hayes and Garfield tried to reform civil service. President Chester Arthur signed an act requiring civil service tests to prove applicants were qualified.

Copyright © by Holt, Rinehart and Winston. All rights reserved.

Interactive Reader and Study Guide

PROGRESSIVES PUSH FOR REFORMS

Progressives were reformers. They wanted to solve problems caused by the fast urban growth of the late 1800s. Journalists wrote articles about such issues as child labor, racial discrimination, and slum housing. Called **muckrakers** for the scandals they exposed, these writers encouraged reforms.

Many progressives helped the urban poor. This led to improved conditions in cities. Other progressive leaders focused on education. States passed laws requiring children to attend school. Kindergartens opened to teach children basic social skills. John Dewey was a supporter of education. His **motive** was to help children use problem-solving skills, not just memorization. Education reform also improved the medical profession.

> **What does the term *muckraker* mean?**
> _____
> _____

EXPANSION OF VOTING POWER

Reformers hoped to expand voting power. They favored the direct primary, in which voters choose candidates directly. They also favored the **Seventeenth Amendment**. This allowed Americans to vote for U.S. senators directly. **Recall** votes removed officials before the end of their terms. In some states voters proposed laws with **initiatives**. Some states let **referendums** overrule laws.

Wisconsin governor **Robert M. La Follette** challenged the power of political machines. His reform plan became known as the Wisconsin Idea, and it was used as a model for reform in other states.

> **What does the Seventeenth Amendment allow Americans to do?**
> _____
> _____

> **Who developed the Wisconsin Idea?**
> _____
> _____

CHALLENGE ACTIVITY

Critical Thinking: Make a Time Line Make a time line of the presidents who served the United States during the Gilded Age.

Copyright © by Holt, Rinehart and Winston. All rights reserved.

The Progressive Spirit of Reform

Section 2

MAIN IDEAS
1. Reformers attempted to improve conditions for child laborers.
2. Unions and reformers took steps to improve safety in the workplace and to limit working hours.

Key Terms and People

Triangle Shirtwaist Fire tragic fire that killed 146 workers

workers' compensation laws laws that guarantee a portion of lost wages to workers injured on the job

capitalism system in which private businesses run most industries and competition determines how much goods cost

socialism system in which government owns and operates a country's industry

William "Big Bill" Haywood union leader of the Industrial Workers of the World

Industrial Workers of the World labor union founded in 1905 on socialist beliefs

Section Summary

IMPROVING CONDITIONS FOR CHILDREN

Reformers also focused on child labor. Children worked in a variety of jobs. Some sold newspapers. Some took care of boarders at their homes. Some sewed clothing. Many worked in industry. Sometimes children as young as seven were sent to work in factories and mills.

Florence Kelley was a reformer who got involved in child labor. She was a board member of the National Consumers' League. The league spoke out on labor issues involving women and children. In 1912 Massachusetts became the first state to pass a minimum wage law. Congress, too, tried to pass laws protecting working children. However, the Supreme Court ruled many of these laws unconstitutional.

> How do you think a minimum wage law helped protect children?
> _____
> _____
> _____

Copyright © by Holt, Rinehart and Winston. All rights reserved.

SAFETY AND WORKING CONDITIONS

Progressives also fought to ensure workers' safety, limit working hours, and protect workers' rights. It took several terrible accidents before laws ensuring workers' safety were passed. One of the worst was the **Triangle Shirtwaist Fire** in New York City. When the factory caught fire, many workers died because factory owners had locked the exit doors.

What finally motivated leaders to pass laws ensuring workers' safety?

Reformers also concentrated on getting **workers' compensation laws** passed. These laws guarantee a portion of lost wages to employees who are injured on the job. Some business leaders believed that the economy should operate without government influence. In *Lochner* v. *New York,* the Supreme Court ruled that states could not restrict the types of labor agreements between employers and employees. The Supreme Court did, however, put limits on the number of hours women and children could work.

What is the purpose of workers' compensation laws?

Labor unions also tried to improve working conditions. Some wanted to take drastic measures, such as changing the economic system of the country to socialism. In **capitalism**, private businesses run most industries and competition determines how much goods cost and how much workers are paid. Under **socialism**, the government owns all the means of production. A new union, based on socialist ideas, was founded in 1905. Under its leader, **William "Big Bill" Haywood**, the **Industrial Workers of the World** hoped to overthrow capitalism. It was not successful and had declined by 1920.

How was the Industrial Workers of the World different from other labor unions?

CHALLENGE ACTIVITY

Critical Thinking: Write to Make Judgments Make a list of the different ways your life would be changed if the reforms discussed here had not happened. Use this list to decide whether or not you agree with the reforms.

Copyright © by Holt, Rinehart and Winston. All rights reserved.

Interactive Reader and Study Guide

The Progressive Spirit of Reform

Section 3

MAIN IDEAS
1. Women fought for temperance and the right to vote.
2. African American reformers challenged discrimination and called for equality.
3. Progressive reforms failed to benefit all minorities.

Key Terms and People

Eighteenth Amendment amendment banning production and sale of alcoholic drinks

National American Woman Suffrage Association group that worked for women's voting rights, founded by Elizabeth Cady Stanton and Susan B. Anthony

Alice Paul founded a women's suffrage group that became the National Woman's Party

Nineteenth Amendment a constitutional amendment giving women the right to vote

Booker T. Washington African American educator who encouraged other African Americans to improve their own lives rather than fight discrimination

Ida B. Wells African American journalist who publicized lynchings in her newspaper

W. E. B. Du Bois African American reformer who publicized cases of racial prejudice

National Association for the Advancement of Colored People organization that brought attention to racial inequality

Section Summary

WOMEN FIGHT FOR TEMPERANCE AND VOTING RIGHTS

New educational opportunities opened up for women in the late 1800s. However, many male-dominated fields were still closed to women. Women's reform groups focused on two issues. One was the right to vote. The other was temperance, for many believed alcohol caused society's problems.

In 1874 the Women's Christian Temperance Union was formed. This group fought for passage of local and state laws restricting alcohol sales. Their efforts were rewarded in 1919 when the **Eighteenth Amendment** banned the production and sale of alcohol.

Meanwhile, women struggled for the right to vote. By 1890 some western states had given women suffrage. That year, the **National American Woman**

> What was the purpose of the Women's Christian Temperance Union?
> _____
> _____
> _____

Copyright © by Holt, Rinehart and Winston. All rights reserved.

Suffrage Association was founded. Reformer Carrie Chapman Catt became its president in 1900.

Alice Paul founded another group that would become the National Woman's Party. It used publicity to draw attention to the issue of suffrage. Paul and other reformers were put in jail. In 1920 the Nineteenth Amendment to the Constitution gave women the right to vote.

> What did the Nineteenth Amendment to the Constitution address?
>
> _____
> _____
> _____

AFRICAN AMERICANS CHALLENGE DISCRIMINATION

African Americans had won their freedom but they still faced discrimination and segregation. African American educator Booker T. Washington urged African Americans to focus on education and economic well-being to end discrimination. Ida B. Wells focused directly on ending discrimination. She told about lynchings of African Americans in her newspaper, *Free Speech*. W. E. B. Du Bois also used publicity to fight racial injustice. He and others founded the National Association for the Advancement of Colored People in 1909 to show the struggles of African Americans. The National Urban League helped blacks find jobs and housing in northern cities.

> Underline the names of all the reformers identified in this section.

FAILURES OF REFORM

Chinese and Mexican immigrants and Native Americans were left out by many reforms. In 1911 the Society of Native Americans was founded to fight Indian poverty. Some Native Americans felt that adopting the ways of whites was destroying their heritage. Chinese immigrants faced discrimination and hard lives. Labor laws did not help Mexican immigrants. They did help the western and southwestern economies.

> List three groups of people that were not generally helped by Progressive reforms.
>
> _____
> _____
> _____

CHALLENGE ACTIVITY

Critical Thinking: Research to Discover Research the Eighteenth Amendment and its repeal. Then write a paragraph about your findings.

Copyright © by Holt, Rinehart and Winston. All rights reserved.

Interactive Reader and Study Guide

The Progressive Spirit of Reform

Section 4

MAIN IDEAS

1. Theodore Roosevelt's progressive reforms tried to balance the interests of business, consumers, and laborers.

2. William Howard Taft angered Progressives with his cautious reforms, while Woodrow Wilson enacted far-reaching banking and antitrust reforms.

Key Terms and People

Theodore Roosevelt vice president who became president upon McKinley's death

Pure Food and Drug Act law stopping the manufacture, sale, or transportation of mislabeled or contaminated food and drugs

conservation protection of nature and its resources

William Howard Taft president elected in 1908

Progressive Party nicknamed the Bull Moose Party; formed so Roosevelt could run for President in 1912

Woodrow Wilson Democratic president who worked to regulate tariffs, banking, and business

Sixteenth Amendment amendment that allows the federal government to impose direct taxes on people's incomes

Academic Vocabulary

various of many types

Section Summary

ROOSEVELT'S PROGRESSIVE REFORMS

Vice President **Theodore Roosevelt** became president when President McKinley was assassinated. Roosevelt was a progressive president. He believed the interests of businesses, workers, and consumers should be balanced, or even sided. This policy was called the Square Deal.

During a 1902 coal miner strike, Roosevelt forced mine managers and strikers to settle their dispute. This was done through arbitration, a formal way of settling an argument. Roosevelt's Square Deal idea helped him win the 1904 presidential election.

> **What did Theodore Roosevelt mean when he used the term Square Deal?**
>
> _____
> _____
> _____
> _____

Copyright © by Holt, Rinehart and Winston. All rights reserved.

President Roosevelt made regulating big business a top goal. Muckrakers helped him by focusing public attention on industry problems. One muckraker, Upton Sinclair, wrote a book on meat processing. The terrible conditions he described led to a meat-inspection law. His book also led to the **Pure Food and Drug Act** of 1906.

Roosevelt was the first president to consider **conservation** an important national issue. Nearly 150 million acres of public land was saved from development under Roosevelt.

> **Why do you think many mining, logging, and railroad companies opposed conservation?**
> _____
> _____
> _____

REFORMS OF TAFT AND WILSON

William Howard Taft became President in 1908 with Roosevelt's support. He felt Roosevelt had more power than the Constitution allowed. So he moved toward reform slowly. **Various** Progressives, including Roosevelt, were not satisfied with some of his reforms. In 1912 Roosevelt ran with the **Progressive Party** against Taft. However, Democrat **Woodrow Wilson** won the election.

> **Why did Theodore Roosevelt form a third party for the 1912 elections?**
> _____
> _____
> _____
> _____

President Wilson immediately began to push for reforms. He was especially interested in tariffs and banking. His tariff reforms led to passage of the **Sixteenth Amendment**. This allowed a direct income tax.

Wilson worked to regulate banking with the Federal Reserve Act in 1913. Passage of the Clayton Antitrust Act and the creation of the Federal Trade Commission helped regulate big business. These programs also helped Wilson win re-election in 1916.

> **What was the purpose of the Federal Trade Commission?**
> _____
> _____
> _____

CHALLENGE ACTIVITY

Critical Thinking: Write to See Connections Write a short paragraph explaining how muckrakers played an important role in the reforms backed by U.S. presidents.

Copyright © by Holt, Rinehart and Winston. All rights reserved.

Interactive Reader and Study Guide

Name _____ Class _____ Date _____

America as a World Power

CHAPTER SUMMARY

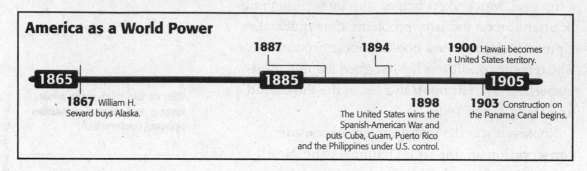

America as a World Power

1887   **1894**   **1900** Hawaii becomes a United States territory.

1865   **1885**   **1905**

1867 William H. Seward buys Alaska.

1898 The United States wins the Spanish-American War and puts Cuba, Guam, Puerto Rico and the Philippines under U.S. control.

1903 Construction on the Panama Canal begins.

COMPREHENSION AND CRITICAL THINKING

As you read the section summaries, fill in the missing information in the time line above and answer the questions below.

1. Identify What important events in this chapter occurred in 1887 and 1894? Add them to the time line above in the correct order.

2. Recall Which island system was the first to fall under U.S. control? Which was the last?

_____

_____

3. Make Inferences When the Spanish-American War ended, Cuba, Guam, Puerto Rico, and the Philippines came under U.S. control. What country controlled them before?

_____

_____

4. Contrast How does the current status of Puerto Rico, Hawaii, and the Philippines differ today?

_____

_____

_____

5. Explain How would the United States benefit from the Panama Canal? How did President Roosevelt gain control of the land to build the Panama Canal?

_____

_____

_____

Copyright © by Holt, Rinehart and Winston. All rights reserved.

Name _____ Class _____ Date _____

America as a World Power

MAIN IDEAS
1. The United States ended its policy of isolationism.
2. Hawaii became a United States territory in 1898.
3. The United States sought trade with Japan and China.

Key Terms and People

imperialism the practice of building an empire by founding colonies or conquering other nations

isolationism a policy of avoiding involvement in the affairs of other countries

William H. Seward Secretary of State who arranged for the purchase of Alaska in 1867

Liliuokalani Hawaiian queen who proposed a new constitution that gave power back to Hawaiians in 1893

spheres of influence areas where foreign nations control trade and natural resources

Open Door Policy policy stating that all nations should have equal access to trade in China

Boxer Rebellion a group of Chinese nationalists that was angered by foreign involvement in China

Academic Vocabulary

process a series of steps by which a task is accomplished

Section Summary

END OF ISOLATION

The decades surrounding 1900 were a time of **imperialism**. During those years, Europeans built great empires by taking control of other lands.

At first the United States followed a policy of **isolationism** and avoided getting involved with the affairs of other countries. That changed in 1867 when Secretary of State **William H. Seward** purchased Alaska. This new territory was a valuable source of fur, minerals, timber, and gold. The United States then took the Midway Islands, part of Samoa, and Hawaii.

> Why would the United States favor isolationism?
> _____
> _____
> _____
> _____

Copyright © by Holt, Rinehart and Winston. All rights reserved.

Interactive Reader and Study Guide

HAWAII BECOMES A TERRITORY

Americans became rich sugar planters, shop owners, and shipyard owners. Sugar became a leading
export in Hawaii. In 1887 the planters forced the
king to sign the Bayonet Constitution that gave
more power to the planter-controlled parliament.
When Queen **Liliuokalani** proposed returning
Hawaii to the Hawaiians, the United States sent
Marines to take control of the islands.

> **How did the United States take control of Hawaii?**
> _____
> _____

UNITED STATES SEEKS TRADE WITH JAPAN AND CHINA

The United States sent Commodore Matthew Perry
to open trade relations with Japan. In 1858 the
United States and Japan signed a trade agreement.
Ten years later, Japanese leaders who favored the
process of industrialization came into power. They
began a 40-year period of change.

The Japanese attacked China and defeated them
in 1894 to became a major world power. Afterwards,
other countries took advantage of China's weakness
to set up **spheres of influence**. To make sure it could
trade with China, the United States announced the
Open Door Policy. This policy said that all nations
should have an equal chance to trade with China.

> **How did Japan become a major world power?**
> _____
> _____
> _____

Chinese resentment grew because the Chinese
did not like being controlled by foreigners. In 1900
this resentment exploded in the **Boxer Rebellion**.
The Boxers attacked the walled settlement in Beijing
where foreigners lived.

> **Why were the Boxers unhappy with foreigners in China?**
> _____
> _____
> _____

For two months the Boxers laid seige to the settlement. Then, military forces from several nations
arrived and defeated the Boxers. China was forced
to pay $333 million to various nations, and the
Open Door Policy remained in effect for years.

CHALLENGE ACTIVITY

Critical Thinking: Write to Evaluate On a map locate the Midway
Islands, Samoa, and Hawaii. Write a paragraph evaluating why the
United States wanted to control these islands.

Copyright © by Holt, Rinehart and Winston. All rights reserved.

America as a World Power

MAIN IDEAS

1. In 1898 the United States went to war with Spain in the Spanish-American War.

2. The United States gained territories in the Caribbean and Pacific.

Key Terms and People

yellow journalism technique that exaggerates and sensationalizes news stories

Teller Amendment war resolution amendment stating that the United States had no interest in taking control of Cuba

Emilio Aguinaldo leader of Filipino rebels against Spain

Anti-Imperialist League organization that accused the United States of building a colonial empire

Platt Amendment amendment to Cuba's constitution that limited Cuba's rights and kept the United States involved in Cuban affairs

Section Summary

WAR WITH SPAIN

During the 1890s Cuba rebelled against Spain, which controlled the island. Many Americans were sympathetic to the Cubans. Two Americans who supported the rebellion were Joseph Pulitzer and William Randolph Hearst. Both men were powerful newspaper publishers. They used **yellow journalism** and published exaggerated stories about the rebellion. This technique sold more newspapers and increased American support for Cuba.

Hearst published a letter in which a Spanish official referred to President McKinley as weak. Many Americans got angry at this insult. Even before that, the U.S. battleship *Maine* had exploded in Cuba's Havana Harbor. No one knew the cause, but many Americans believed that Spain was responsible.

In response, the U.S. Congress declared that Cuba was an independent country. They also passed the **Teller Amendment**, which stated that America would not take control of Cuba. Spain immediately

> Why did publishers such as Pulitzer and Hearst resort to yellow journalism?
> _____
> _____
> _____
> _____

Copyright © by Holt, Rinehart and Winston. All rights reserved.

Interactive Reader and Study Guide

declared war on the United States, and fighting began in Cuba.

Fighting in the Pacific at the same time, the U.S. Navy destroyed Spain's fleet in the Philippines. Filipino rebels led by **Emilio Aguinaldo** and U.S. troops took control of Manila, the capital.

Other U.S. troops focused on the Caribbean Sea. These troops included the Rough Riders, led by future President Theodore Roosevelt. After the United States won battles both on land (in Cuba and Puerto Rico) and at sea, Spain surrendered.

> Why was the war fought in the Pacific as well as in Cuba?
>
> _____
>
> _____

UNITED STATES GAINS TERRITORIES

The peace treaty with Spain put Cuba, Guam, Puerto Rico, and the Philippines under U.S. control. A group of Americans formed the **Anti-Imperialist League**. They were afraid the United States wanted to build an empire and deny self-government to people in the territories. Despite their work, the treaty passed.

> Why would Filipinos want to help the United States fight the Spanish?
>
> _____
>
> _____
>
> _____

The United States set up a military government in Cuba. It added the **Platt Amendment** to Cuba's new constitution. This allowed the United States to stay involved in Cuba's affairs and limited Cuba's right to make treaties. The amendment remained in force until 1934. The United States stayed active in Cuban affairs until the late 1950s.

> Why did many Americans oppose the U.S. control of more land?
>
> _____
>
> _____
>
> _____
>
> _____

The United States decided to keep the Philippines and Puerto Rico as territories. Puerto Ricans became U.S. citizens in 1917. Today Puerto Rico has its own constitution, but it is still associated with the United States. Filipinos fought America for their independence, and hundreds of thousands died. In 1902 Congress established an appointed governor and elected legislature in the Philippines. The country became independent in 1946.

CHALLENGE ACTIVITY

Critical Thinking: Write to Compare Write a paragraph that compares the purpose of the Teller Amendment with the purpose of the Platt Amendment.

Copyright © by Holt, Rinehart and Winston. All rights reserved.

Interactive Reader and Study Guide

America as a World Power

MAIN IDEAS
1. The United States built the Panama Canal in the early 1900s.
2. Theodore Roosevelt changed U.S. policy toward Latin America.
3. Presidents Taft and Wilson promoted U.S. interests in Latin America.

Key Terms and People

Panama Canal canal built in Panama that shortened the Atlantic-to-Pacific voyage

Roosevelt Corollary President Theodore Roosevelt's warning that nations in the Western Hemisphere should pay their debts and "behave"

dollar diplomacy President William Howard Taft's policy of influencing governments through economic intervention

Mexican Revolution rebellion against Mexican president Porfirio Díaz

John J. Pershing United States general who pursued Pancho Villa through Mexico but never caught him

Francisco "Pancho" Villa rebel leader during the Mexican Revolution

Academic Vocabulary

role assigned behavior

Section Summary

BUILDING THE PANAMA CANAL

A canal across Central America would cut 8,000 miles off a voyage between the East and West U.S. Coasts. It would link the country's naval fleets. When Theodore Roosevelt became president, he tried to get Colombia to lease land in Panama for a canal. Colombia rejected the idea.

When Panama revolted against Colombia in 1903, a U.S. warship blocked Colombian forces from reaching Panama. The rebels won, and Panama declared itself independent. Then the United States and Panama agreed to build a canal.

Many lives were lost to disease and dangerous working conditions during the construction of the **Panama Canal**. Despite these dangers it opened to ships in 1914.

> Why would foreign nations be interested in building a canal through Central America?
> _____
> _____
> _____
> _____

Copyright © by Holt, Rinehart and Winston. All rights reserved.

U.S. POLICY TOWARD LATIN AMERICA

In 1823 President Monroe warned European nations to stay out of the Western Hemisphere. The Monroe Doctrine became a major part of U.S. foreign policy until 1904. When Theodore Roosevelt became president, he wanted the United States to play a more active **role** in the Western Hemisphere.

By the early 1900s several Latin American nations owed money to European investors. Roosevelt warned these nations that if they did not pay their debts, the United States would step in. The **Roosevelt Corollary**, an addition to the Monroe Doctrine, also gave the United States "police power" in the hemisphere.

> How is the Roosevelt Corollary related to the Monroe Doctrine?
> _____
> _____
> _____

U.S. INTERESTS IN LATIN AMERICA

President William Howard Taft tried **dollar diplomacy**. This was a way to influence governments by economic, instead of military means. President Woodrow Wilson did not like the role of big business in foreign affairs. He ended the use of dollar diplomacy and sent troops to protect U.S. interests in Latin America.

> What would be an advantage of dollar diplomacy over military intervention?
> _____
> _____
> _____

In 1910 the **Mexican Revolution** caused the overthrow of the government. The violence of the revolution caused many Mexicans to flee to the United States. It also upset American business leaders who had investments in Mexico. President Woodrow Wilson requested and received from Congress permission to use force against Mexico.

> Underline the sentence that states why many Mexicans moved to the United States in the early twentieth century.

Wilson sent General **John J. Pershing** and 15,000 soldiers into Mexico to catch **Francisco "Pancho" Villa**, the rebel leader. Villa had killed 17 Americans in New Mexico. Pershing and his troops never caught Villa. In 1917 a new constitution started to bring order to Mexico.

CHALLENGE ACTIVITY

Critical Thinking: Write to Sequence Write a paragraph that relates the attempts U.S. presidents made to control Latin America.

Copyright © by Holt, Rinehart and Winston. All rights reserved.